CW01335989

Alfred Lord Tennyson

Twayne's English Authors Series

Herbert Sussman, Editor

Northeastern University

TEAS 525

ALFRED TENNYSON
Photograph from the Tennyson Research Centre, Lincoln, by permission of Lincolnshire County Council.

Alfred Lord Tennyson

The Poet in an Age of Theory

W. David Shaw

University of Toronto

Twayne Publishers

New York

Twayne's English Authors Series No. 525

Alfred Lord Tennyson: The Poet in an Age of Theory
W. David Shaw

Twayne Publishers

1633 Broadway
New York, New York 10019

Library of Congress Cataloging-in-Publication Data

Shaw, W. David (William David)
   Alfred Lord Tennyson : the poet in an age of theory / by W. David Shaw.
      p.   cm. — (Twayne's English authors series : no. 525)
   Includes bibliographical references and index.
   ISBN 0–8057–4577–7 (cloth : alk. paper)
      1. Tennyson, Alfred Tennyson, Baron. 1809–1892—Criticism and interpretation.
2. English poetry—19th century—History and criticism—Theory, etc.   I. Title.
II. Series: Twayne's English authors series : TEAS 525
PR5588.S47   1996
821'.8—dc20   96–12869
                                                                      CIP

The paper used in this publication meets the minimum requirements of American National Standard for Information Sciences—Permanence of Paper for Printed Library Materials, ANSI Z39.48-1984. ∞ ™

10 9 8 7 6 5 4 3 2

Printed in the United States of America

Contents

Preface

Drawing upon recent literary theories to elucidate neglected aspects of Tennyson's achievement, this book substantiates T. S. Eliot's claim that Tennyson "has three qualities which are seldom found together except in the greatest poets: abundance, variety, and complete competence."[1] I use recent feminist theory to show how comic and heroic modes in *The Princess* and high rhetoric and plain speaking in "Demeter and Persephone" and "Oenone" confer power on women speakers. With the help of Nina Auerbach's monograph, *Private Theatricals: The Lives of the Victorians,* I also distinguish between staged and real deaths in Tennyson's elegies. Mieke Bal's idea of a "mirror-text" is used to show how Tennyson's resourceful deployment of frames and fragments shapes his experiments with poetic narrative. Eric Griffith's theory that a silent reading of many Victorian poems creates dramas for the eye and ear that are unavailable in an oral recitation is also tested in a close reading of Tennyson's monologue, "Ulysses." Finally, I revive Helen Vendler's concept of the "reinvented poem" to study Tennyson's composition of a palimpsest of texts, in which traces of alternative versions are allowed to shine through.

Using Richard Wollheim's distinction between "acting" a dramatic part and "acting out" a fantasy,[2] the book explains why Tennyson is only a moderately successful playwright yet a brilliant writer of dramatic monologues. Arguing that a monologue like "St. Simeon Stylites" is better designed to explore the psychology of martyrdom than stage plays like *Becket* and *Queen Mary,* in which martyrdom is a major theme, I work toward a new understanding of the dramatic monologue and of Tennyson's achievement in that genre.

The book is the first monograph to demonstrate that Tennyson's monologues trespass on intimacies of consciousness and free vagrancies of mind that are unavailable in other poetic genres. By examining fantasy and bad faith in Tennyson's monologues, and by showing how monologues make us intimate with speakers unsuited for their roles, the book advances a new theory of the most innovative poetic genre of the nineteenth century.

Though it may be currently unfashionable to say so, I believe that readers in an age of theory can still benefit from a humane, experience-based study of Tennyson's life-long experiments with poetic language and genre. Celebrated in his own time as an ornate poet, Tennyson is also a master of the sublime. I show how *Maud* and *In Memoriam* alternate between an expansive and an elliptical use of sublime language. Few poets are more daring and resourceful than Tennyson in disturbing and transforming the genres they inherit. And few look deeper into the abyss in things. In confronting the void Tennyson often imparts a tremor to his verse by using two-way syntax, indefinite or late-breaking caesuras, and forms of grammatical hovering. In a deconstructionist reading of *Idylls of the King,* I argue that we miss the point of the *Idylls* if we fail to see that one of the targets of their two-way meanings is the moral authority of Tennyson himself. Perhaps it is only Tennyson's sympathy for a reader's desire for coherence that prevents his deconstructing morality all the way down. After showing in other poems how Tennyson explores the allegiances of a self-divided mind by setting speech slightly at odds with lyric form, I demonstrate how his allusions to Milton, Spenser, Wordsworth, and Keats, far from being conventional imitations, are innovative speech acts, fully "performative" in J. L. Austin's sense of that word.

A bibliographical essay at the end of the book traces recent developments in Tennyson scholarship and criticism. After assessing the scholarship of Tennyson's recent biographers and editors, including the editors of Tennyson's letters, I review the contributions to Tennyson studies of feminist criticism, the new historicism, deconstruction, and some contemporary theories of language.

Chronology

<table>
<tr><td>1809</td><td>Born at Somersby, Lincolnshire, on August 6, 1809, the third of eleven children. Son of Rev. George Clayton Tennyson, who had been forced into the church when displaced by his rich father in favor of a younger son.</td></tr>
<tr><td>1820–1827</td><td>The poet's father educates his sons at home in Latin and Greek and encourages the poetic compositions of the three older boys. But when the father's suicidal alcoholism drives him to bouts of insane violence in the 1820s, the young poet throws himself on a grave in the churchyard and prays for his own death.</td></tr>
<tr><td>1827</td><td>Poems by Two Brothers published by a provincial printer in the spring of 1827. None of Tennyson's contributions to the volume are included in his authorized canon. Admitted to Trinity College, Cambridge, on November 9, 1827.</td></tr>
<tr><td>1829</td><td>Meets Arthur Hallam, son of the historian Henry Hallam, with whom he develops a swift and deepening friendship. Joins a talented society of Cambridge undergraduates, the "Apostles," and wins the Chancellor's Gold Medal for his prize poem, "Timbuctoo."</td></tr>
<tr><td>1830</td><td>Publishes Poems, Chiefly Lyrical. Accompanies Hallam on a trip to the Pyrenees, where he gives money and moral support to the Spanish rebels.</td></tr>
<tr><td>1833</td><td>Death of Arthur Hallam in September, 1833. Hallam, who had been engaged to marry Tennyson's sister, had been loved and needed as much by the poet and his sister as they had been loved and needed by him.</td></tr>
<tr><td>1834</td><td>Falls in love with the rich Rosa Baring, who rejects him as a social inferior. Both beyond his reach and beneath his love, Rosa continues to exert an important influence on "Locksley Hall" and Maud.</td></tr>
<tr><td>1842</td><td>Publishes Poems (1842). Volume one is a selection from earlier books, including many creatively revised poems.</td></tr>
</table>

Volume two is a selection of new poems. They establish Tennyson as the leading poet of his generation.

1847   Publishes *The Princess*, which sells better than any of Tennyson's previous books, but which disappoints Carlyle and Fitzgerald. For many modern readers only the poem's exquisite songs and lyrics survive. If a chronology of Tennyson's life begins to look like a bibliography, it is because Tennyson's life is a private one: there is a sense in which his biography *is* his bibliography.

1850   Tennyson's *annus mirabilis*. Publishes *In Memoriam*, his greatest poem and the major poetic document of the Victorian age. The same year brings his long-postponed marriage to Emily Sellwood and his appointment as Poet Laureate, a successor to Wordsworth.

1855   Publishes *Maud*, a poem of madness, suicide, and family feuds that tries to exorcise some of the bitter experiences of Tennyson's first four decades. Even after he is married, famous, and outwardly secure, Tennyson remains one of William James's "second-born" spirits. His mastery of neurosis and grief is always precarious and fraught with risks.

1859   Publishes the first books of *Idylls of the King*, which continue to appear over the next twenty-six years. Though these poems extend Tennyson's reputation in both Britain and America and enjoy some critical esteem, they are attacked in their own time by Carlyle, Browning, Swinburne, Hopkins, and Meredith, and have enjoyed a mixed critical reception ever since.

1875   From 1875 onward Tennyson writes plays, including *Queen Mary*, *Becket*, and *The Foresters*, which are produced with moderate success.

1883   Gladstone persuades Tennyson to accept a peerage. With increasing prosperity and fame, the poet comes to live the last part of his life as a national and international institution.

1886   Death of Lionel, the poet's younger son. Obscurely feeling he has failed Lionel, Tennyson complains to his older son, Hallam, that "the thought of Lionel tears me to pieces—he was so full of promise and so young."

1887   Tennyson writes "Demeter and Persephone," the great classical monologue of his old age, and during the 1880s continues to write with affectionate tact such epistolary masterpieces as his lines "To the Marquis of Dufferin and Ava" and his verse letter "To E. Fitzgerald."

1892   When Tennyson dies on October 6, 1892, at the age of eighty-three, the most representative interpreter of his great and troubled era, he is borne to Westminster Abbey amid more pomp and ceremony than ever accompanied an English writer.

PART ONE
Genres in the Making

Tennyson follows the Romantic poets, especially Wordsworth, in what one critic, F. E. L. Priestley, calls a "new and freer attitude towards genre."[1] Just as Wordsworth in his *Lyrical Ballads* yokes two genres, the lyric and the ballad, which earlier poets found incompatible, so Tennyson continually blends or fuses epic, elegiac, and satiric genres in new and surprising combinations. In his narrative poem *The Princess*, he wants to discover how far he can combine heroic and comic modes, and how far the pastoralism of Theocritus and Ovid can be assimilated to epic and even tragic moods. In *In Memoriam* and the lines "To the Marquis of Dufferin and Ava" Tennyson tries to accommodate elegy's high style and decorum to a diary's informalities and to the intimacies of a verse epistle. He also challenges the norms of epic poetry by showing in *Idylls of the King* how casuists like Guinevere and tricksters like Vivien live on the borderland between falsehood and truth. Even through their evasive tropes and babbling lips the oracle may be heard.

In the first part of this monograph I examine how the inevitable intrusion of the prosaic domestic world into the world of epic and elegy unsuits speakers for the high rhetoric and ceremony that these genres traditionally demand of them. As political injustices create powerful off-key effects, the Poet Laureate may even find himself increasingly alienated from the glories of empire he is called upon to celebrate. Like his poems of politics and state, many of Tennyson's most famous narrative poems, elegies, and Arthurian idylls are really generic experiments in disguise. By experimenting with "mirror-texts" and frames, and by showing how even adulterers like Lancelot and Guinevere cannot help reflecting a fragment of the truth they also subvert, Tennyson disturbs and transforms the genres in unexpected ways.

Chapter One

Tennyson's Narrative Frames and "Mirror-Texts"

Because Tennyson's gift is for lyric rather than narrative poetry, he is constantly wrestling with the necessary angel of continuity. When composing longer poems he keeps experimenting with frames and embedded texts that can mirror his overall design while releasing the mind from narrative constraints. Such frames and fragments are themselves sub-species of the genre that Mieke Bal has called the "mirror-text,"[1] a synec-dochic narrative that uses part of a story to represent the whole. If a pan-theist like Spinoza were to write poetry, his "mirror-text" might be Blake's "Auguries of Innocence"—

> To see a World in a Grain of Sand
> And a Heaven in a Wild Flower
> Hold Infinity in the palm of your hand
> And Eternity in an hour
>   ("Auguries of Innocence," ll.1–4)

—or Tennyson's "Flower in the Crannied Wall," lyric fragments that boldly equate microcosm and macrocosm:

> I hold you here, root and all, in my hand,
> Little flower—but *if* I could understand
> What you are, root and all, and all in all,
> I should know what God and man is.
>   ("Flower in the crannied Wall," ll.3–6)[2]

The shocking solecism of Tennyson's final phrase, which uses a singu-lar verb for a plural subject, memorably affirms the power of a "mirror-text," not only to use the part to represent the whole, but also to iden-tify many properties with a single substance. Though we may only half understand Tennyson's "mirror-text," our incomprehension is part of its meaning. The smallest flower or leaf has power to utter something stupendously direct and important: only our prodigious stupidity has prevented our hearing or understanding what the oracle has said.

A "mirror-text" may "bare the device," as the Russian formalists say, or tip the poet's hand, by disclosing for an instant a poem's secret spring or genesis. Such a "mirror-text" can be found in canto 4 of the second part of *Maud*, the lament "O that 'twere possible" (II.141–238), where a lyric of loss, originally composed in 1837 for Arthur Hallam, reveals how the whole poem, like a pearl grown from a grain of sand, has organized itself around a germinal fragment.

> O that 'twere possible
> After long grief and pain
> To find the arms of my true love
> Round me once again!
>
> When I was wont to meet her
> In the silent woody places
> By the home that gave me birth,
>
> We stood tranced in long embraces
> Mixt with kisses sweeter sweeter
> Than anything on earth.
> (*Maud*, II.iv.141–50)

The association of this fragment with *In Memoriam* discloses in a flash that the speaker's love for Maud has its origin, not just in Tennyson's unrequited love for Rosa Baring, but also in his deeper love for Hallam, whose gender has been switched in the poet's narrative displacements of a lyric impulse.

The framing "Prologue" of *The Princess* presents the story of a summer gathering at a Victorian country estate: seven men agree to entertain the company with stories embedded in the framed fabula, while the women sing ballads or songs. Young Walter of the "Prologue" is recognizable as Florian in the fabula, and the maiden aunt Elizabeth as Lady Blanche: Lilia mirrors the Princess and the narrator the Prince. Embedded in this "Prologue" is another mirror-text, a "gallant glorious chronicle" recounting the exploits of Sir Walter's ancestor, Sir Ralph, whose mock-epic tone is replicated in the main story.

> 'O miracle of women,' said the book,
> 'O noble heart who, being strait-besieged
> By this wild king to force her to his wish,
> Nor bent, nor broke, nor shunned a soldier's death . . .
> ("Prologue," *The Princess*, ll.35–38)

By the time the chronicle's epic invocation is repeated thirteen lines later, however, its truth has begun to effervesce. Who can describe as "noble" or "miraculous" the Britomarts who push men from rocks and drown them in whirling brooks?

As in a dream vision by Chaucer, where the prologue's events undergo dreamlike transformations in the framed narrative, Tennyson's "Prologue" dexterously mirrors the many tonal shifts in the medley that makes up the main story. The natural appeal of Vivian-place is more than just a triumph of gadgetry. The splendor of the "fire-balloon" that rises "gem-like up before the dusky groves" (ll.74–75) is not quite canceled out in irony. Its "fairy parachute" exerts some of the pastoral poem's traditional charm, which is one of the minor marvels of the "Prologue."

If Vivian-place, like Ida's college, is absurd, its vision of a world of noble manners and actions is also more than absurd. Even as Tennyson pokes fun at the giddy girls, "dislinked" from their circle "with shrieks and laughter" by an "electric shock" (ll.69–70), he makes us feel strongly the charm to eye and ear of the "gilded ball" and "rain of pearls" (ll.62–63). As a mirror-text, the "Prologue" is easier to interpret than the story it frames. Though the trivial amusements are faintly absurd, the humor is qualified by countervailing impressions of a beautiful pastoral world where young men and women may still live in harmony with their surroundings and in accord with each other.

Just as Sir Walter, the landscape-improver and patron of the village, whose minor errors of taste can be overlooked as harmless luxuries, is more than a parody of the medieval host, so Ida is more than a caricature of embattled womanhood, a "feudal warrior lady-clad" (l.119). By presenting a less sympathetic version of the main narrative, the embedded story of the Prologue may even make Ida appear more appealing when we finally meet her. At Vivian-place, "universal culture for the crowd" (l.109) verges on parody of the democratic ideal. Student pranks and gossip about tutors also represent a sad decline from Renaissance theories of a prince's education. The "Prologue" contrasts such perversions of the educational ideal with Ida's college, which revives Roman heroism and education in ancestral civic virtues even as it dedicates itself to renewing and living out the rights of the liberated woman.

In Tennyson's elegies the mirror-text and the primary text often change position. Ostensibly, both the dedicatory epistle and the postscript to the monologue "Tiresias" are poetic frames. But for those readers to whom the problems raised in the monologue are more compelling than Tiresias' answers, the postscript provides a more effective resolution. As the frame to a monologue that urges us to face death bravely, the postscript for Edward Fitzgerald, who had died before the monologue and its prefatory epistle could be sent, tests even Tennyson. So affecting is the postscript, which seems dictated, not by art, but by life, that the picture space and frame begin to switch places. A framed text that rings throughout with the finality of death slowly comes to mirror the even more remarkable poem that frames it.

In focusing on Tennyson himself, as the frame at the end of "Lycidas" focuses on Milton, the postscript relates death to personal motives. In the bleak memory of "so many dead, / And him the last" ("To Edward Fitzgerald," ll.82–83), Tennyson's postscript seems to be going to pieces, breaking with grief for a final time. But the end of the poem possesses the authority that comes from having gone through great disorder, then coming out again on the other side.

> What life, so maimed by night, were worth
>   Our living out? Not mine to me
> Remembering all the golden hours
>   Now silent, and so many dead,
> And him the last; and laying flowers,
>   This wreath, above his honoured head,
> And praying that, when I from hence
>   Shall fade with him into the unknown,
> My close of earth's experience
>   May prove as peaceful as his own.
>   ("To E. Fitzgerald," ll.79–88)

As the last lines of the postscript look forward to the poet's own death, and complete what we understand to be, in every sense, a last farewell, it is no longer the shock of Fitzgerald's death that surprises, but the elegance and ease with which the postscript absorbs that shock. So surprising is the frame's perfect control of disaster in an imperfect world that it overshadows and absorbs everything else in the poem.

A comparable exchange of picture space and frame occurs in Tennyson's verse epistle to James Spedding. The primary loss is the death of Spedding's brother, Edward, who died in his youth. But the narrative of another death, which Tennyson uses to frame the poem's ostensible subject, increasingly preoccupies the elegist.

> Alas!
> In grief I am not all unlearned;
> Once through mine own doors Death did pass;
> One went, who never hath returned.
>
> He will not smile—not speak to me
> Once more. Two years his chair is seen
> Empty before us. That was he
> Without whose life I had not been.
> ("To J.S.," ll.17–24)

As Tennyson continues to draw a circle of words around his loss, not naming his father directly but inviting the reader to solve a little riddle, he also broods upon a second clue and puzzle: why "Those we love first are taken first" (l.12). Just when the frame around the main picture, which is the emptiness created by his father's death, seems to be all but forgotten, it returns with unexpected force to fill up the whole picture space of the poem.

> In truth,
> How *should* I soothe you anyway,
> Who miss the brother of your youth?
> Yet something I did wish to say:

> For he too was a friend to me:
>   Both are my friends, and my true breast
> Bleedeth for both; yet it may be
>   That only silence suiteth best.
>   ("To J.S.," ll.57–64)

The moment the thought of his father's death becomes the elegy's implicit subject rather than its mirror-text or frame, it takes all his heart for speech. Any thought he can voice about his loved but doomed father, the alcoholic rector, will violate the primal silence of the family. And unlike the elegy he has written, which is remarkable for the honesty with which it charts the truth of the poet's feelings, any spoken tribute would almost certainly be a lie.

The most common mirror-texts in Tennyson are framed narratives, where a story is told in one or more embedded texts. The classic examples are *The Princess*, "Morte d'Arthur," "The Gardener's Daughter," and "The Sleeping Beauty," where narration occurs at several levels. The narrative frame in "Morte d'Arthur" is part of Tennyson's own protective strategy: by allowing Edward Hall, the author of the embedded Arthurian story, to joke about the epic he has burned, the frame allows Tennyson to voice and deflect criticisms of his own epic experiment before readers have a chance to make similar objections themselves.

To give his primary narrative in "Demeter and Persephone" a contemporary interest, Tennyson even embeds inside the great earth mother's apocalyptic coda (ll.126–36) her millennial hope of breaking "The sunless halls of Hades into Heaven" ("Demeter and Persephone," l.134), a prophecy more biblical than pagan. As Tennyson explains, "when I write an antique like ["Demeter and Persephone"] I must put it into a frame—something modern about it. It is no use giving a mere *rechauffé* of old legends."[3]

In a domestic idyll of complex narrative framing, "The Gardener's Daughter," it is difficult to tell which story forms the primary narrative and which story is embedded as its mirror-text. At first we assume that the framing narrative is the story of Eustace's portrait of his fiancée, Juliet. When Eustace insists that the ideal artist is Love, and that only an adoring painter can produce a perfect portrait, he seems to be mirroring the moment at the idyll's center when the speaker falls in love with the gardener's daughter, whom he sees framed on her cottage porch by an Eastern rose: "Half light, half shade, / She stood, a sight to make an old man young" (ll.139–40). Though Tennyson said that because this framing narrative is "the Centre of the poem, it must be full and rich,"[4] we are surprised to learn in the narrative's concluding frame that the speaker is not addressing us directly. He is addressing an unknown auditor "to whom," as Dwight Culler notes, "the portrait is being unveiled by the speaker years after his beloved's death."[5]

Should we follow Tennyson's advice to treat the real portrait as the one created in words rather than paint at the center of the poem? Or, since Rose's death and the idyll's status as a dramatic monologue are finally revealed in the closing frame, should we not demote Rose's framing at the poem's center to just another mirror-text, like Eustace's painting of Juliet in the opening frame? The poem's surprise ending suggests that we may have mistaken the shifting relations of the main narrative to its two embedded texts, just as we have mistaken the poem's genre. If so, the idyll is a dramatic monologue in disguise, and the words addressed to the unidentified auditor to whom the speaker finally unveils the dead woman's painting are not a mere concluding frame, but the principal story after all. The multiple frames lead simultaneously *toward* and *away* from the void at the center of the speaker's life and poem.

Like the gardener's daughter, Tennyson's Sleeping Beauty is embedded within several framed narratives of her own wooing. Because even the primary narrative of the fairy tale is presented in separate frames, three magic casements seem to open up, like windows of an Advent calendar, at the center. In this faery land forlorn, sensations of grief, awakening life, and the fullness of love seem capable of being presented only in a distant and formal medium, corresponding to the distancing frame at the end of Keats's "The Eve of St. Agnes."

> And they are gone: ay, ages long ago
> These lovers fled away into the storm.
> ("The Eve of St. Agnes," ll.370–71)

Like Keats, Tennyson's speaker has to find a dramatic tale of fulfilled love as far away as possible from his own fond feelings for his present auditor, Lady Flora, and yet intimately in touch with them.

> 'A hundred summers! can it be?
> And whither goest thou, tell me where?'

> 'O seek, my father's court with me,
>   For there are greater wonders there.'
> And o'er the hills, and far away
>   Beyond their utmost purple rim,
> Beyond the night, across the day,
>   Through all the world she followed him.
>   ("The Departure," ll.25–32)

The three panels of life-conferring action at the tale's enchanted center, in which the Prince beautifully completes the rite of passage that is sadly aborted in "The Lady of Shalott," are immediately preceded by two static pictures of the Sleeping Beauty and her frozen Palace. The true "mirror-text," however, is removed to the periphery of these five central panels: it is to be found in the "Prologue" of "The Day-Dream" and also in the poem's three concluding frames, "Moral," "L'Envoi," and "Epilogue," which keep signaling closure without actually concluding anything.

The elaborate nesting structure of these frames inside frames creates an infinite regress, or *mise en abyme*, a term deriving from heraldry, where the recursive effect occurs in pictorial representations. But the more these frames multiply, the more they both approach and retreat from a set of tactfully coded instructions to Lady Flora about how to interpret the fairy tale. At first the poet is reluctant to append any moral to his frames: he insists that we profane art, the "wildweed-flower that simply blows," whenever we stoop to truth and moralize our song ("The Moral," l.6). But as the reserve of the art critic gives way to intimacy, even urgency, the speaker reveals in his two concluding frames that he has an ulterior motive, half sportive, half earnest, in allowing his mirror-texts to produce recursive effects long after the story should formally conclude.

> For since the time when Adam first
>   Embraced his Eve in happy hour,
> And every bird of Eden burst
>   In carol, every bud to flower,
> What eyes, like thine, have wakened hopes,
>   What lips, like thine, so sweetly joined?
>   ("L'Envoi," ll.41–46)

As a secret admirer who wants to play Prince Charming to Lady Flora, the speaker combines a poet's whimsy with a lover's talent for paying gracefully oblique compliments. Reluctant to force a conclusion, the speaker allows his poem to wander on, like a vagrant dream, beyond its anticipated closing frame. As the "L'Envoi," which usually signals closure, is followed by an unexpected "Epilogue," the poet uses his mirror-text to urge his beloved to look into her own mirror and whisper, without vanity, "What wonder, if he thinks me fair?" ("Epilogue," l.4). The speaker's daydream, we discover, is a masked love poem. Continuing to disturb and transform his genre, Tennyson uses the contrivance and disguise of a fairy tale to achieve a slow but sure progression in intimacy.

In *Idylls of the King*, which also contains a number of "mirror-texts," the embedded fables are designed not so much to explain the primary narrative as to resemble it. Though the explanations in these embedded texts are usually merely hinted at, they retain the advantage of freeing the mind from narrative constraints by using dream visions, prophecies, or riddles to present the main story in embryo, or else to compress it into some odd cryptogram or code.

Like Cathy's dream of being homesick in heaven in *Wuthering Heights*, which Nelly is reluctant to hear because she knows dream visions have their own frightening potency, Leodogran's vision in "The Coming of Arthur" enjoys prophetic authority precisely because it *is* a vision. In Leodogran's mirror-text Tennyson lays out the double nature of Arthur's kingship: on the one hand, the inevitability of mortality and death in the apparition of a phantom king who is powerless to stay the burning and the slaughter; on the other hand, the sense of Arthur's permanence when, in the midst of a dissolving world, he comes to tower magisterially over everything else in the idyll.

> and thereon a phantom king,
> Now looming, and now lost; and on the slope
> The sword rose, . . .
> Till with a wink his dream was changed, the haze
> Descended, and the solid earth became
> As nothing, but the King stood out in heaven,
> Crowned.
>
> ("The Coming of Arthur," ll.429–43)

Like many mirror-texts, this passage does not seem adequate to its narrative function. Leodogran has been trying to judge Arthur's claims. Why should his vision of Arthur's impotence as a phantom king help Leodogran resolve his doubts by deciding in Arthur's favor? In a strict psychological sense, the power of an impotent king is an absurd idea, or at best a paradox. But Tennyson uses the passage as a mirror-text. He wants to illustrate the cyclical pattern of history, which demands Leodogran's replacement now, as it will demand Arthur's later. Like the primary narrative of *Idylls of the King*, this embedded text is a summary statement of time's dominion over kings. By enacting historical pathos, it places the problem of succession in a wider context of human feeling about time, the great destroyer, which first annihilates loyalties, then the lives of men, and finally "the solid earth" itself, which becomes "As nothing."

The coherence of *Idylls of the King* is not one of narrative consistency. It is rather a coherence of feelings and attitudes of the kind we find in Merlin's puzzling song.

> "Rain, rain, and sun! a rainbow in the sky!
> A young man will be wiser by and by;
> An old man's wit may wander ere he die.
> Rain, rain, and sun! a rainbow on the lea!
> And truth is this to me, and that to thee;
> And truth or clothed or naked let it be.
> Rain, sun, and rain! and the free blossom blows:
> Sun, rain, and sun! and where is he who knows?
> From the great deep to the great deep he goes."
> ("The Coming of Arthur," ll.402–10)

Composed in units of three (in triple rhymes, in the three semantic units of each triplet, and in the arrangement of three words, "Rain, rain, and sun" to form three distinct chains: AAB, ABA, and BAB), the lyric affirms patterns that are as prophetically obtrusive as the oracular repetition of the phrase: "The old order changeth, yielding place to new" ("The Coming of Arthur," l.508; "The Passing of Arthur," l.408). But like the *Idylls* as a whole, these patterns also affirm a purely formal order in excess of any clear conceptual one. Though nurtured by sun and rain, the origin and destiny of the freely blowing blossom are as mysterious as the rainbow's origin, and they prompt Merlin's question: "where is he who knows?" The transit from "the great deep to the great deep" affirms an order, but one whose meaning—even at the end of the *Idylls*—is never clear to anyone. As a true prophet, Merlin refuses to answer our questions. He offends against epic norms by withholding the insight he seems to offer.

Like the narrative in which it is embedded, Merlin's mirror-text is both hopeful and disillusioned. The young man's wisdom is qualified by the old man's senility, and the availability of truth is canceled by its very relativity: "And truth is this to me, and that to thee." As an old man's wandering wits disclose that normal assumptions of cause and effect are arbitrary and vulnerable, the reader's momentary feeling of knowing more than Merlin gives way to an unsettling sense of the essential sanity of the magician's prophecies and the madness of more commonplace minds. Just as our ordinary assumptions are dissolving, the affirmation of order in the journey from "the great deep to the great deep" makes us feel as lost and lonely as Merlin.

As in Carlyle's *Sartor Resartus*, every intimation of unmediated presence has its countervailing intimation of absence or nothingness: "But whence?—O Heaven, whither? Sense knows not; Faith knows not; only that it is through Mystery to Mystery, from God to God."[6] Like Carlyle, Tennyson repeats Schiller's critique of Western man's infatuation with some absolute proximity of voice and being. From the first idyll of the poem, we sense that Tennyson is no longer in possession of any norm of vision. Unlike the God who makes himself "an awful rose of dawn" in "The Vision of Sin" (l.224), Tennyson cannot control what is seen. Instead, he is a reluctant deconstructionist, impelled to strip away the veiling fictions, but afraid to face what his stripping will disclose. Like fleeting images seen in a mirror, Leodogran's dream and Merlin's riddle provide only elusive and vanishing glimpses of the truth. Whereas the traditional epic poet holds a mirror up to nature, the mirror-texts of the *Idylls'* prophets and seers are designed to show that, far from being a simple object of knowledge, truth is relational: as Fichte argues, it is something uniting the objective world with ourselves.

In "The Lady of Shalott" the mere presence of a mirror helps readers identify a mirror-text. When Lancelot is said to flash into the Lady's crystal mirror from "the river," the double nature of that mirroring— from bank to river to mirror—turns the water's reflecting surface into a second mirror (ll.104–6). The multiple distancing of the world outside the tower is itself a mirror-text. It resembles the primary narrative of the world seen by the Lady of Shalott "moving through a mirror" in part 2. And it also helps explain the meaning of this mirroring by associating it with Plato's cave, where everything is seen at one remove from its source, like shadows on a wall.

A metafiction is a mirror-text that comments, often obliquely, on the artistry of the work in which it appears. In an elaborate metafiction in Tennyson's stage play, *Becket*, the anticlerical Map seizes on Becket's jibe that the Pope's kindling may end in smoke. Instead of mounting straight up, the Pope's smoke "is fain to diagonalise." Becket professes to despise this "diagonalizing" and jokes about the barbarous neologism. But because "strange diagonal," the subtitle of Gerhard Joseph's first book,[7] is a phrase Tennyson himself had used to describe the narrative method of *The Princess*, Map's satire is as much a joke at Tennyson's expense as at the Pope's.

> And I, betwixt them both, to please them both,
> And yet to give the story as it rose,
> I moved as in a strange diagonal,
> And maybe neither pleased myself nor them.
> (*The Princess*, "Conclusion," ll.25–28)

Walter Map: "Nay, my lord, take heart; for though you suspended your-self, the Pope let you down again; and though you suspend Foliot or another, the Pope will not leave them in suspense, for the Pope himself is always in suspense, like Mahound's coffin hung between heaven and earth—always in suspense, like the scales, till the weight of Germany or the gold of England brings one of them down to dust—always in sus-pense, like the tail of the horologe—to and fro—tick-tack—we make the time, we keep the time, ay, and we serve the time;

> (*Becket*, Act II, scene 2, Vol. 9, pp. 113–14)

"Suspend" in the sense of "censor or disallow" alternates with the literal meaning of "leave hanging." By allowing his triple use of the phrase "in suspense" to hang suspended, Tennyson not only uses the idea that he mentions but also revives its forgotten figurative force. Though comic in context, the speaker who defers outcomes by hovering in space is exper-imenting with a device Tennyson himself develops into one of his poetry's most distinctive features.

To "affect" like Becket "the unwavering perpendicular" is to search irritably after facts that refuse to formulate. It is also to reject negative capability and Tennyson's own happy aptitude for syntactic wavering and delay, as in the stream's timorous advance and retreat above the waterfall in the proem to "The Lotos-Eaters."

> And like a downward smoke, the slender stream
> Along the cliff to fall and pause and fall did seem.
> ("The Lotos-Eaters," ll.8–9)

In its resourceful hovering, the "mirror-text" in *Becket* identifies an important feature of Tennyson's own capacity to hover at the brink, not just in "The Lotos-Eaters," but also in a monodrama like *Maud*, where wavering and delay dramatize the uncertainty of a mind vividly and mysteriously at conflict with itself.

Often Tennyson uses narrative frames to dramatize his belief that the minimal unit of cognition is always, in the words of his friend J. F. Ferrier, the Scottish idealist, the object framed by a self-conscious subject, "the thing, or thought, *mecum*."[8] Tennyson's theory of knowledge is, like Ferrier's, an epistemology of frames. Each time the mind perceives something, one of the things it affirms is its own marriage, its own indissoluble union, with the world it perceives. And what God has joined together, let no man put asunder! In passing "Into the Nameless, as a cloud / Melts into heaven" ("The Ancient Sage," ll.233–34), the human consciousness is simply showing that its capacity to frame the world reflexively is one more token of the Nameless's much greater capacity to do the same thing.

As Tennyson's version of Wallace Stevens's paradox that "the absence of the imagination had / Itself to be imagined" ("The Plain Sense of Things," ll.13–14), his monologue "Mariana" shows how self-consciously framed absences like the absent visitors who lift the latch or the absent lover who sighs like the wind can be more vividly realized than items perceived directly through the senses. We are taught to prize as a prerogative of the mind an ability to withdraw from the tyranny of unmediated impressions and to make framed absences more real than unframed sensations. Indeed Tennyson believes, with George Berkeley and J. F. Ferrier, that unframed sensations are a contradiction in terms, because like the falling tree in the earless forest, the only reality is what a framing mind (God's or our own) *perceives* to be real: *esse est percipi*.

Sometimes, as in section 101 of *In Memoriam*, where Tennyson anticipates a scene of neglect and oblivion after his family leaves Somersby and

the garden-boughs and flowers fall into ruin, the negative past participles, moved ominously to the head of poetic lines—"Unwatched,"
"Unloved," "Uncared for"—start to toll like a knell, momentarily
detaching the blank mirror of nature from a framing consciousness.

> Unwatched, the garden bough shall sway
>
> (l.1)

> Unloved, the sunflower, shining fair
>
> (l.5)

> Unloved, by many a sandy bar,
> The brook shall babble down the plain
>
> (ll.9–10)

> Uncared for, gird the windy grove
>
> (l.13)

Tennyson's anxiety may also be felt in his uneasy syntax: "And year by
year our memory fades / From all the circle of the hills" (ll.23–24). Is the
possessive pronoun "our" a subjective or objective genitive? Does the
poet's memory of the hills fade, or the hills' memory of *him*?

The second possibility is the more unexpected and disturbing. And
yet even the hills' fading memory of the poet is a framing of the past
that the poet himself has still to enclose inside a second frame. Because
Tennyson, even in grieving that the life of significant soil is no longer
loved and cared for, continues to love and care for it, he expects us to see
why no mirroring of place, however bleak, can be unhinged from the
memorial or testament of a self-conscious mind. In framing the hills'
power to frame the disappearance of Tennyson and his family from the
Somersby rectory, even the poet's imagination of oblivion powerfully off-
sets the bleakest impressions of loss.

Chapter Two

Heroic and Comic Modes:
Feminism in *The Princess*

Unlike the weak and subservient Amelia Sedleys and Agnes Wickfields of Victorian fiction, the women in Tennyson's monologues are often strong and liberated. Even when abandoned and betrayed, Oenone and the southern Mariana achieve an illusion of strength by swearing revenge and by serving as oracles in whom dream vision and prophecy take place. More liberated than either of them is the heroine in Tennyson's narrative poem, *The Princess*, who founds a college for feminists. Combining heroic and comic modes, the poem both defends and makes fun of Victorian feminism.

Princess Ida's liberation is compromised by multiple ironies. Even in issuing her edict against talking to men, she breaks it by speaking to disguised male intruders. In taking us on a tour of her gallery of statues, Ida celebrates the heroic status of women. Like the female soul in her Palace of Art, however, or the Lady of Shalott, the feminist's strength is most apparent when she resolves to leave her ivory tower for more adventurous living in a world which sanctions a desired play of male and female contaries. Though the play of opposites may lead to tyranny, without contraries self-growth would be limited.

Also more enlightened than the male chauvinist in "Locksley Hall," who proclaims that women are inferior and unequal to men, is Tennyson's Prince, who affirms the sexes are equal. Because the Prince also acknowledges their differences, however, he seems out of step with some modern feminist criticism, which insists that men and women are soul-mates: men should have qualities of compassion and fellow-feeling too often ascribed exclusively to women, and women should have courage and strength of mind, attributes too often limited to men. In "On One Who Affected an Effeminate Nature," Tennyson deplores the behavior of gynandrous men and androgynous women. But he also endorses the goal of many feminists in announcing that "while man and woman still are incomplete, / I prize that soul where man and woman meet" (ll.1–2). If androgyny is defined as a union of masculine and feminine traits, then Tennyson can be said to favor androgyny as a transgression of gendered boundaries.

In toppling the too-familiar marriage plots of social fiction, *The Princess* tells what one critic, in speaking of Charlotte Brontë's *Shirley*, calls an "incompleted story of female bonding," upon which the more traditional and "artificial edifice of heterosexual courtship"[1] has been imposed. Constantly alternating between high epic seriousness and comic plain speaking, the Princess is torn between principle and practice, between feminist ideology and the play of sexual impulse. In appropriating the male prerogatives of academic study, self-confident oratory, and political power, and in denouncing the vivisectionists for "carving the living hound" (III.293), Ida is less an object of satire than an advocate of just causes, far ahead of her time. Heroically solemn about her feminist crusade, she can also laugh at her own vaunted imperviousness to sex:

> when we set our hand
> To this great work, we purposed with ourself
> Never to wed.
>
> (II.45–47)

Her "great work" remains studiously vague. There is a flavor of mystery about its exact meaning.

Tennyson deftly balances absurdities in the Princess with qualities that are immensely appealing. The perversely arch and sexually ambiguous heroine is a familiar character in Victorian fiction, where she appears as Isabel Archer in *The Portrait of A Lady* and as Dorothea Brooke in *Middlemarch*—women who are married to an ideology rather than a man. While her college's "lucid marbles" and "ample awnings gay" (II.10–11) compose a poetry of luxury and well-made objects, the simile comparing the brightly dressed intruders to "rich moths" emerging from "dusk cocoons" (II.5) gives the reader an exquisite sense of the precious slightness of the rituals. Tennyson preserves the splendor of the "Academic silks" (II.2), but the essence of his wit lies in the beautiful diminution. Ida is a kind of marvelous sophomore; man's role is to be docile; and the innate foolishness of that teaching, while no more ludicrous than the opposite doctrine of male superiority, provokes the Prince's amusement and irony. Though there is a school-girl vagueness about the Princess, who yearns for something larger than people or society, she also expresses the values of a world where feminist crusades are serious matters.

The formality of Ida's welcome deviates into momentary comedy as the heroine who boasts that her visitors may someday attain her own epic stature recognizes with a slight shock that the disguised Prince and his fellows are taller than she is. Ida declines to play child's games, because she has solemnly renounced the "tricks" that make women "toys of men" (II.49). Denouncing male stereotypes of women, she invokes an epic muster roll of proper names to draw attention to the college's collection of female statues. The gallery of statues celebrates, not sleek slaves of the harem nor stunted squaws, but female warriors, architects, and legislators.

> Look, our hall!
> Our statues!—not of those that men desire,
> . . .   but she
> That taught the Sabine how to rule, and she
> The foundress of the Babylonian wall,
> The Carian Artemisia strong in war,
> The Rhodope, that built the pyramid,
> Clelia, Cornelia, with the Palmyrene
> That fought Aurelian . . .
>
> (II.61–70)

It is hard to dissociate the heroic celebration from a touch of vanity in the connoisseur of art objects. Ida displays a pride of ownership, like an art collector taking us on a tour of her favorite pieces. Epic conventions also blend incongruously with traditions of that seventeenth-century literary genre, the "gallery," in which historical or mythical figures appear in a series of prose or verse portraits, a tradition Tennyson had already used in "The Palace of Art." The promiscuous blending of women athletes, warriors, and legislators is about as stripped and quintessential as the clutter of relics at Vivian-place, the country estate of Sir Walter, which is described in the "Prologue" with an irony that is coolly remote and finely ambiguous.

Like Ida's decree forbidding conversation with men for three years, which is undone at the moment it is reaffirmed, her high epic manner is constantly implying some light-hearted criticism of the persons and customs she celebrates. As high rhetoric turns to plain speaking, even the private jokes and awkward silences of her auditors prevent Ida's language from deviating into simple solemnity. When she derides male chauvinism and the arrogance of women's "self-styled . . . lords" (II.51), the Prince and his comrades keep the tone light and humorous by betraying their embarrassment as they stare studiously at the matting.

In her welcome to the disguised male intruders, Ida opens at the top of the tonal scale, with a formal salutation that redounds more to her own self-importance than the credit of her coterie. By the end of the passage she descends from the overpitch of the heroic style to semi-vulgar colloquialisms that satirize Lady Psyche's lecture as a "harangue" and the college itself as a hive of bees. Ida's decorum easily embraces a variety of moods: high declamation, both laudatory and satirical; remembered scenes and tirades; and a serious and elitist tone of self-praise, manifestly oratorical, that allows Tennyson to refashion epic in Ovidian terms. The pointed antitheses and balanced rhythms make the heroic mode at once more solemn and amusing than anything found in his earlier verse.

Throughout *The Princess* Ida alternates oddly between tender melancholy and cold declamation. Her lofty rhetoric conveys a strong sense of asserted will and a resolve to be free. But when she comes to surrender Psyche's child (VI.175–90), the telling points of the lofty polemical style slip into a confused tangle of ambiguous feeling, in which the cold brilliance of the orator is both warmed and dimmed.

The decline of heroic rhetoric into vulgar, self-serving speech is most comical in Lady Blanche, who talks of the purity of nature, public welfare, and vengeance all in the same breath. Her confusion emerges most clearly when she threatens to drag her child away, implying she has supported the college for selfish motives.

> Thereat the Lady stretched a vulture throat,
> And shot from crooked lips a haggard smile.
> 'The plan was mine. I built the nest' she said
> 'To hatch the cuckoo. Rise!' and stooped to updrag
> Melissa.
>
>   (IV.344–48)

The combination of high purpose and low motive is beautifully traced in the swing from grandiose claims about dedication and self-sacrifice to the colloquial simplicities of a beast fable. Like Ovid's heroines,

Tennyson's are wonderfully agile in pleading their cases and scoring points: "And since my oath was ta'en for public use, / I broke the letter of it to keep the sense" (IV.318–19). These comic shifts from high rhetoric to plain speaking express Tennyson's delight in the tangle of human motives and the mingled charm and absurdity of rival claims.

When Ida surrenders the child to its mother, the reformer's heroic resolve betrays a new simplicity and tenderness: "Pretty bud! / Lily of the vale! half opened bell of the woods!" (VI.175–76). The sylvan flower's reclusiveness mingles incongruously with the declamations of the feminist, who must still campaign aggressively in a public forum. So sustained is the playing off of impulses that the ambiguous tumult in her heart becomes all but satirical. Like her oxymoron of a "yoke . . . Gentle as freedom" (VI.188–89), the heroine's optatives verge on paradox: "may thy mother prove / As true to thee as false, false, false to me!" (VI.186–87). As figures of antithesis and contradiction mount to near hysteria, automatically tripling the adjective "false," the harsh successive stresses of Ida's declamation begin to slide into parody and burlesque. These impressions are confirmed a moment later when Gama denounces the heroine as a monster of cruel vanity and monstrous whim.

> ·   no heart have you, or such
> As fancies like the vermin in a nut
> Have fretted all to dust and bitterness.
>   (VI.245–47)

In this biting piece of wit any impression of the heroine's charm or nobility is deftly deflated. Ida seems consistent now only in her preposterous egotism, expressing itself in every extreme of passion and "wild whim" (l.226).

When Ida recovers her composure, however, she expresses a more balanced attitude in a conciliatory address to Psyche. Now the high rhetoric of the epic mode, with its exalted sense of the heroine's mission and fame—"I should have had to do with none but maids, / That have no links with men" (VI.273–74)—alternates with a plainer, more intimate style capable of expressing genuine love for Psyche.

> Come to the hollow heart they slander so!
> Kiss and be friends, like children being chid!
>   (VI.270–71)

The simple candor makes it easier for Ida and Psyche to make up their differences. To be rebuked and reconciled is the proper end of a children's quarrel. But their conflict is also sharpened by balanced phrasing and alliteration, which shape their female bonding into perfectly matching units of sound and sense.

> Ah false but dear,
> Dear traitor, too much loved, why?—why?—
>   Yet see,
> Before these kings we embrace you yet once more
> With all forgiveness, all oblivion,
> And trust, not love, you less.
>
> (VI.274–78)

Skillfully broken by dashes to give the impression of agitated, impromptu speech, the chiasmus and paradox ("Ah false but dear, / Dear traitor, too much loved") are more than rhetorical tricks, since they aptly characterize a heart in conflict. The paradox of a "nightmare weight of gratitude" (VI.281) and her fine distinction between continuing to love Psyche but ceasing to trust her (VI.278) dramatize a perilous affinity between feelings of being intimate and being betrayed.

Still unable to see that falling in love with a man may not be a fall from grace but a growth in understanding, Ida uses satiric conceit and word play to mock her mingling with "The soft and milky rabble of womankind, / Poor weaklings . . . as they are" (VI.290–91). Though Ida's capacity to love both men and women is not impaired by her power to be discriminating, her interplay of high rhetoric and plain speaking takes her on a roller-coaster ride that plummets down one steep emotion only to soar up its opposite on the other side.

Later, in pleading with the Prince to forgive her (VII.212–30), Ida's astonishingly harsh judgment of herself runs a gamut of emotion. Starting from a low point of humiliation and shame, she mounts to a plateau of irony and hauteur, where she discerns the larger truth that "something wild within her breast, / A greater than all knowledge, beat her down" (VII.222–23). But then her heroic manner falters, and she subsides again into half-comic colloquialism and self-doubt, mocking herself as "a Queen of farce" (VII.228).

Though the Princess can still not see how two lives may be shared without being sacrificed or wholly merged, she comes increasingly to resemble the woman in her song, "Ask me no more" (VI.364 ff.), who, though resisting love, is also dying of it. Ida's speaker repeats the words "Ask me no more," not to tranquilize, but to charge the phrase with more and more feeling. The content of the phrase changes from threat of refusal in the first stanza to uncertainty in stanza two to imminent surrender at the end. The surprising force of the lyric comes partly from metrical bareness and partly from the swift progression in intimacy, focused in the change of epithets: "fond," "friend," "dear love" (ll.4, 8, 14).

The penultimate lyric in *The Princess* confirms Ida in her newfound love. In "Now sleeps the crimson petal" (VII.161–74), one of the most exquisite lyrics ever written, the lover becomes more a seer than a painter of landscape, and under his eye a marvelous transformation takes place. In an unbroken, chainlike process of visual mergings, the beloved, the meteor, and the stars join together in cosmic space, with the lover as one of the marveling participants. But the true marvel comes with the merging of objects, when the blending becomes so complete that the lily is lost entirely in the lake. In the penetration of the male form by the lily, Tennyson transgresses gendered boundaries. The receiving element is first equated with the woman—"the Earth all Danaë" (l.167) to the shower of stars—and then, in a sexual reversal, with the man, "the bosom of the lake" that enfolds the lily (l.172). By the end of the lyric, opposites no longer consciously embrace but slip into each other, lost in a coupling of pronouns—"my dearest, thou" (l.173)—and a grammatical identity of persons. Even the microscopic charm of the winking "fin" and "fire-fly" (VII.163–64) are beautifully fused in images that join heaven and earth and approximate in words a water-lily painting by Monet.

The most perfect blending of high rhetoric and plain speaking occurs during an interval of life-giving illumination and insight when the Prince appeals to Ida during his illness.

> 'If you be, what I think you, some sweet dream,
> I would but ask you to fulfil yourself:
> But if you be that Ida whom I knew,
> I ask you nothing: only, if a dream,
> Sweet dream, be perfect. I shall die tonight.
> Stoop down and seem to kiss me ere I die.'
>
> (VII.130–35)

The prayer is affecting because it asks for nothing. If Ida's apparition *is* a dream, then it may with propriety be asked to fulfill itself. Like Keats's image of the sleeping Adam, the Prince hopes to wake from his dream to find it true. Though the prophecy of his death makes his beloved's gesture of seeming to stoop down and kiss him a felicitous gesture, it is still valedictory and funereal. More desirable, though still beyond his power to understand or take for granted, is his imagination of being restored to health by his beloved's appearance, not in mere make-believe or dream, but in a real-life drama of resurrection and rebirth.

If this is Ida, and not some apparition in a dream, then her very appearance is reward enough. Before he literally breathes his last, he will die as lovers die when they consummate their love. The pathos of the speech lies in the modesty of the lover's request: "I ask you nothing," and in the tender distancing of the auxiliary verb of illusion, "seem to kiss," which makes the lover think his bliss is too exquisite to be real. This is the kind of moment we remember and treasure in *The Princess*. The language of dream vision is exalted and heroic, but it is also touched to poetry by the plainness at the heart of an ordinary domestic situation. The Prince speaks with the simplicity of a child awakening from a life-threatening illness, and consoled by the presence of a ministering angel, part soul-mate and part mother.

We have shared Tennyson's delight in the absurdities of passion masquerading as idealism and political highmindedness. Now we discover that it is hard to surpass him in the expression of life-giving desire. Because neither the Princess nor her lover is using words for rhetorical effect, but like a kiss or a touch, the scene acquires something of the subtle scope and feel of a rebirth. Though the expression of intense physical passion lies outside the range of *The Princess*, the Prince's invocation to Ida, which is reminiscent of Lear's invoking Cordelia as a guardian angel after her return from France, shows how Tennyson can still maintain high epic decorum while using odd plain words ("I would but ask you to fulfil yourself") to explore subtle states of renewal and desire. This is the most moving moment in the poem, not because it fulfills some feminist agenda, but because the Prince has no time to reassemble his sense of self and the politically correct language that goes with it. Since Ida and the Prince are no longer talking past each other, this is the one time in the poem their words and feelings wholly coincide.

Chapter Three

Poems that Disturb
or Transform Their Genres

It might be argued that all Tennyson's poetry aspires toward the condition of elegy. The poet laureate of politics and state is a self-critical patriot. He is not just celebrating Britain's greatness: he is also composing elegies for its decline. Similarly, *Idylls of the King* is less a heroic celebration of Arthurian Britain than a prolonged lament for its fall. In this section I want to suggest how Tennyson disturbs and transforms the conventions of the Arthurian epic and the ceremonial or political poem, and how he also transforms the conventions of elegy itself, which he often uses to refashion the other poetic genres.

Like Marvell in his Horatian ode to Cromwell and Pope in his "Epistle to Augustus," Tennyson subverts the platitudes of ceremonial tribute by making it impossible to dissociate criticism from praise in his finest poetry of state. In his "Ode on the Death of the Duke of Wellington," for example, the sententious identification of "The path of duty" with the "way of glory" (l.210) cannot quite disguise oddities in the account. Certain lines waver, expressing the lapse into doubt. And submerged metaphors of darkness, death, and gloom increasingly obsess Tennyson. The probability of God's accepting Wellington, and of Christ's receiving him, depends on the preceding hypothesis that the duke is "Something far advanced in State" (l.275). The pun on "State" shows how skeptical, how playfully subversive the poet laureate remains, willing to change a premise as soon as he entertains it. As in the ceremonial music of another laureate of empire, Sir Edward Elgar, a heroic melancholy sounds softly but incessantly in the empty spaces of the ode—in the drum roll of its triple rhymes and the ground swell of its caesural pauses and strongly end-stopped lines.

> Hush, the Dead March wails in the people's ears;
> The dark crowd moves, and there are sobs and tears;
> The black earth yawns: the mortal disappears;
> ("Ode on the Death of the Duke of Wellington," ll.267–69)

The second thoughts and qualifications that abound in Tennyson's
ceremonial poems are also evidence of an unwillingness to falsify belief.
Halfway through "A Welcome to Her Royal Highness Marie
Alexandrovna" (1874) the glories of state suddenly strike the poet as too
overwhelming. Though he feels the grand fulfillment of history in the
marriage ceremony, his wavering caesural pauses keep miming the
tremulous hopes of fame's aspirants: history's "thrones and peoples are as
waifs that swing, / And float or fall, in endless ebb and flow" (ll.26–27).

Equally unstable are the glories of empire in the ode "On the Jubilee
of Queen Victoria" (1887). Opening with two fearful questions—"Are
there thunders moaning in the distance? / Are there spectres moving in
the darkness?" (ll.66–67), the last six lines, allegedly added at Victoria's
request, try to veil Tennyson's fears by slipping into religious exhortation: "Trust the Hand of Light will lead her people" (l.68). As Tennyson
comes to grip with his fear, he shifts without warning from the subjunc-
tive "pass" and "vanish" to two present indicatives:

> Trust the Hand of Light will lead her people,
> Till the thunders pass, the spectres vanish,
> And the Light is Victor, and the darkness
> Dawns into the Jubilee of the Ages.
> ("On the Jubilee of Queen Victoria," ll.68–71).

The ode implies that desire has at last found its object in a Jubilee whose
dawning literally "dawns" at the head of a new poetic line. But the
unstable grammar also resembles the quicksand of empire, and alerts us
to the possibility of being deceived about the light, whose dawning may
be a mere trick of language.

"Till," followed by two present tenses, signals a future in disguise.
The grammar can imply either the endless present of celestial time or,
alternatively, a visionary hope that may never be realized—an equivocation on which Tennyson relies. Looking forward to Victoria's death, his
appeal to the Second Coming, when the darkness will dawn "into the
Jubilee of the Ages" (l.71), rejects the secular terms on which the whole
ode has been constructed. Such a rejection is common enough in satirical
or elegiac verse, in a poem like Pope's "Epistle to Augustus," which values the monarch George II only when his "suns of glory" will have "set."
But in Tennyson's case the nominal subject of his ode—the greatness of
secular empire—has changed to imperial gloom, with the result that the
poem we think we are reading turns into something else.

A proper reading of Tennyson's ode "The Charge of the Light Brigade" (1854) must include both the heroic celebration of the slaughtered patriots and the implicit rebuke of the "one" who "had blundered" (l.12).

> When can their glory fade?
> O the wild charge they made!
> All the world wondered.
> Honour the charge they made!
> Honour the Light Brigade,
> Noble six hundred!
>
> ("The Charge of the Light Brigade," ll.50–55)

As Anglo-Saxon monosyllables combine with a sonorous drum roll of dactyls to evoke a precipitate descent into "the valley of Death," it is easy for a reader to be lulled into uncritical acceptance of the carnage. But just when the celebrant's mind is being numbed by the heroic muster call, his critical faculties return to check the drift into reverie. Two gaping metonymies, "the jaws of Death" and "the mouth of Hell" (ll.46–47), remind us that the charge is "wild" in a double sense (l.51)— both brave and reckless.

Anyone who has heard Tennyson recite "The Charge of the Light Brigade" in an old recording will remember how its headlong lines are pulled into the orbit of chant and incantation. Wrenched from horror or plaintiveness, the poet seems to be going through a half-magical routine. Instead of tranquilizing him, however, his broad Lincolnshire accent charges the vowels with more and more feeling. As in Yeats's poem "Easter 1916," a "terrible beauty" attaches to the "Noble six hundred," not because they belong to a class of special people but because they represent the special class of martyrs. Their "glory" would be less inviolable if it were not so arbitrary.

Tennyson's reverence for the English constitution, like his reverence for Camelot, is inspired by a Burkean vision of civilized order, a contract between the living, the dead, and those yet unborn. Though this view of history and society would have been fully intelligible to Aquinas and Hooker, as it was to their nineteenth-century counterparts, Coleridge and Matthew Arnold, it would probably have seemed reactionary to liberals like Godwin and Shelley. With his conservative Burkean faith in civilized order, however, Tennyson (who owned an eight-volume edition of Edmund Burke's works) manages to combine a radical belief in progress.

Confident that human nature is perfectible, J. S. Mill develops the political philosophy of Godwin and Shelley into the official Victorian creed that social truth will spread. In "Locksley Hall" Tennyson appears to endorse this creed. His political imagination is stirred by the young speaker's Utopian vision of a "Parliament of man, the Federation of the world" (l.128).

> There the common sense of most shall hold a fretful realm in awe,
> And the kindly earth shall slumber, lapt in universal law.
> ("Locksley Hall," ll.129–30)

Combined, however, with the counter-vision of a lion's slow encirclement of a dying campfire (ll.135–36), the verb "slumber" is disturbing. Like Godwin, the youth in "Locksley Hall" dwells in the fond haven of an unreal paradise. As a triumph of millennial hope over sober expectation, his Godwinian political beliefs are already fading into an uneasy dream.

As theories of progress give way in nineteenth-century thought to theories of random process, Tennyson fears that society may develop haphazardly. His political poetry is therefore of two kinds: a poetry of official apology like "Love Thou Thy Land" (1842), written from a sense of belonging to an elect people, and a poetry of foreboding like the Jubilee odes, which disengage themselves from the partisanship of empire and party. In the second kind of poetry, especially in the disturbing prophecies of "Locksley Hall Sixty Years After" (1886), which his friend Gladstone resented, Tennyson discloses that he has less in common with Queen Victoria and such imperialists as the Marquis of Dufferin than with Thomas Hardy and Henry Adams, thinkers who are profoundly anxious about the non-teleological implications of Darwin. For the aging Tennyson the evolutionary escalator is no longer a smoothly rising "altar-stairs / That slope through darkness up to God" (*In Memoriam*, 55.15–16) but a wild, careening roller coaster, doubtfully teleological and frightening to contemplate.

In replacing a heroic celebration of Camelot with a long and sustained elegy for it, *Idylls of the King* also disturbs and transforms the epic genre. Tennyson's Arthurian poem has less in common with Miltonic, Spenserian, or Virgilian epic, or even with Malory, than with such Victorian fictions as *Vanity Fair* and *Middlemarch*. Like Thackeray, Tennyson writes an epic narrative without a hero; or at the very least, he redefines the meaning of heroism, as George Eliot does in the prelude and finale of her "home epic," *Middlemarch*.

In *Idylls of the King* the sweep of a conventional epic action acquires a different kind of amplitude: it survives, not in the expanse of an epic narrative, but in the inclusiveness of its readers' sympathies and fears. In "The Passing of Arthur" readers are aware from the inside of everything going on in the minds of Arthur and Bedivere. But they are equally aware of what Guinevere and Lancelot experience. In a Gothic world where the living stagger and the dead walk, we share intimacies of consciousness with the dying Galahad and the defeated Arthur that we also share with such agents of destruction as Guinevere and Lancelot.

Epic narratives conventionally trace a spiral. Though Milton's Adam and Eve are expelled from Eden, they find a "Paradise within [them], happier far" (*Paradise Lost*, 12.587) than that which they have lost. Aeneas loses Troy but wins glory as the founder of Rome, a new and greater Troy. *Idylls of the King* disturbs this epic convention by presenting two disparate sides to time: linear and circular. For Camelot and the knights of the Round Table time has an arrow. The collapse of their early idealism into the disillusion and cynicism of "The Last Tournament" is complete and irreversible. Like the Second Law of Thermodynamics, which makes time move in one direction only, this linear vector arouses anxiety because it points towards the end of time and the world.

But countering this linear arrow is Merlin's vision of Arthur's passing to come again and the reappearance of the three queens at the hour of Arthur's death. For the tragic arrow of time Tennyson substitutes, not the spiral action of Virgilian or Miltonic epic, which is both linear and progressive, but the comfort of a nontemporal cycle, where the past is the future because there is no real history, only an interval between two eternities: "From the great deep to the great deep he goes" ("The Passing of Arthur," 1.445).

The built-in contradiction of a temporal model that possesses the same contradictory circular and linear attributes as *Idylls of the King* reappears as the celebrated irreversibility paradox of nineteenth-century physics, formulated in 1876 by Loschmidt. "The apparent time reversibility of motion within the atomic and molecular regimes, in direct contradiction to the irreversibility of thermodynamic processes," where time is one-directional, "suggests that the two great edifices—

thermodynamics and mechanics—are at best incomplete."[1] We have to
say of *Idylls of the King* what Loschmidt says of time itself, that its structure is both circular and linear. Because Tennyson cannot reconcile these
two views of time in the traditional epic figure of the spiral, his poem
retains the historical pathos of a world that, even in tracing out circular
designs, remains one-dimensional and linear.

Idylls of the King is far closer in spirit to the Arthurian poems of
William Morris than to Malory's narratives. Unlike Malory, Morris and
Tennyson summon up Arthurian phantoms that pass stormfully across
the earth before dissolving like ghosts into the unknown. The silence at
the end of Morris's "The Defence of Guenevere," for example, when the
queen refuses to speak another word but turns sideways to listen for
Lancelot, is truly a void. Like the closing words of "The Holy Grail," "So
spake the King; I knew not all he meant" (l.916), the absence of any
answer is as audible as a gong.

What Morris, like Tennyson, tries to capture in the unheard words that
are forever rising to the surface of his Arthurian poems is death the void,
the absence of consciousness. When Morris's Galahad hovers on the edge
of oblivion, the poetry's imperfect rhymes—"weary," "Miserere"—and
strong seventh-syllable caesuras drift into easeful death with him.

> Right so they went away, and I, being weary,
> Slept long and dream'd of Heaven: the bell comes near,
> I doubt it grows to morning. Miserere!
>   ("Sir Galahad: A Christmas Mystery," ll.150–52)

The words *are* what they say, a drift into oblivion, and as such mimetic.
But they are also *anti-mimetic*, a presentational assault on mimesis, since
the subsiding cadences are actually the unspoken subject, which keeps
rising to the surface of the poem, becoming indistinguishable from the
flagging metrical pulse which all but stops at the late-breaking caesura,
barely able to sustain its beat to the end of the line.

If Morris's Guenevere, like Tennyson's, moves her auditors, it is not
by her arguments but by the inspired simplicity of her language.

> "Do I not see how God's dear pity creeps
> All through your frame, and trembles in your mouth?
> Remember in what grave your mother sleeps, . . ."
>   ("The Defence of Guenevere," ll.151–53)

By rotating the simple sounds—"creeps," "tremble," "Remember"—
she imagines what is otherwise beyond imagining, the "dear pity"
of God and the severed head of her accuser's brutally murdered
mother. The "awful drouth / Of pity" which "drew" that "blow" is not so
much a trope as a rotation of sounds that turn the speaker slowly toward
death.

Like his poetry of state and his ghostly Arthurian narratives,
Tennyson's elegies continue to disturb and transform generic norms. The
Greek elegists commemorate the permanence of an objective order of
nature, set against the transience of man. *In Memoriam* produces a seis-
mic shock by transgressing this code: instead of being stable and enduring, nature is as much in flux as man. For John Keble the book of nature
is a second Scripture, a medieval Book of Hours. For Tennyson in *In
Memoriam* it is a mere book of moments, a spectacle of Heraclitean transience and flux. In laying the foundation for the conquest of Darwinian
science, Charles Lyell, Robert Chambers, and their contemporaries had
done an extraordinary thing. They had formulated a third-person system
of the world that had all the disadvantages of being impersonal without
any of the advantages of being stable. Removing one of the norms of the
ancient Greek elegists, accidental variation had fashioned a natural order
in which the scientists themselves could no longer find a meaningful
place.

Elegy is always "in memoriam": an art of re-viewing and recollecting
the past, as opposed to merely remembering it. Yet Tennyson also transgresses this convention by reminding us, often with a slight shock of
recognition, that elegy is equally an art of forgetting. Indeed, until the
mere impact of a sensory impression of the dead is effaced, until the dead
are forgotten, they cannot be genuinely recalled either. Recollection is an
art; and, as Kierkegaard observes, "what is recollected is not indifferent
to recollection as what is remembered is indifferent to memory."[2]
Without recollection there could be no meditation, and without meditation no discovery and growth.

The impulse toward coherence and stability in literature and politics,
toward remembering a past they want to conserve, is deeply rooted in
the consciousness of Tennyson's mourners. But faced with the unknown,
they also waver between hope and fear. Having destroyed something,
like radicalism in politics, can death put something better in its place?
Whatever one's politics, death the leveler is always a highly visible radical. A constant reminder of human equality, it is also the great trans-
gressor of norms.

Because individual lyrics of *In Memoriam* have all the lapidary concision of epitaphs, they seem to meet one of classical elegy's most important norms: they achieve a maximum cathartic effect with a minimum of material. Even after finishing a short elegiac monologue like "Ulysses" or "Tithonus," we may feel we have been through a tragic drama, so concentrated and cathartic is the experience. But the more of *In Memoriam* we read, the more we realize that it also violates this norm. The long elegy seems endlessly to end, and so never ends at all, except by a kind of optional stop rule that says, "now we shall have an epithalamium that writes 'finis' to our story." *In Memoriam* transgresses its genre by emulating a Gothic fiction's unholy amalgam of marriage and metamorphosis. Its protean changes of form are as capricious as they are sublime: "The hills are shadows, and they flow / From form to form, and nothing stands" (123:5–6). The undirected metamorphic energy of Tennyson's elegy might never cease if terminal events like the marriage of his sister Cecilia to Edmund Lushington did not set their own evolutionary seal on the poetry's impulse to explode, change course, or simply dissolve into fragments.

Locked in the grip of his stupor and incomprehension, the mourner in *In Memoriam* seems not to understand the nature of playing a mourner's part. He is unaware of the repertoire of roles available to the pastoral elegist. Nor does he seem any more familiar with the conventions of the confessional elegy, a genre that in poems like Donne's *Anniversaries* might have supplied him with stabler compass points or resting places.

Anything sententious that is said about the nature of mourning in this elegy, about rising on stepping stones of our dead selves or about moving toward some far-off divine event, seems wrong or off-key. The elegist has made us so intimate with the inarticulateness and stupor of his grieving that he must forgo the consolations of comprehension and renewal. It is as anomalous for the reserved, inarticulate elegist of *In Memoriam* to write an elegy as it is for an autobiographer who says his secret is his own ("Secretum meum mihi") to write *Apologia Pro Vita Sua*. Tennyson writes a long elegy that amplifies and extends his grief instead of mastering and subduing it. But the more he reveals the more he also withholds. A grievously reticent mourner, Tennyson believes that a consolation expressed is usually a lie. What a mourner genuinely feels, he does not express: and what he expresses tends to falsify what he feels.

By establishing a decorum of indecorum, a pun like "The far-off interest of tears" (I.8) allows the mourner to evoke a real sense of uncertainty from a real experience of it. Despite what is said about "a use in measured language" (V.6), the incessant motions of the mourner's "unquiet heart and brain"(V.5) never quite conform to any pattern. Just when the mourner's mind seems poised on the threshold of a unifying perception, the impingement of a new frame of reference frustrates his attempt to specify the particular coherence his mind now grasps. Since he is unable to realize the precise nature (and so the precise limits) of his grief, it is already on its way to becoming a "divine despair."

Though the elegy combines formal, logical, and syntactical structures, as well as many phonetic and figurative patterns, none of these structures is aligned in a concerted phalanx: sometimes they work together, but often they pull apart. While the two middle lines of each stanza contract the meaning, the first and fourth lines tend to diffuse it. In section IX, for example, lines 14 and 15 are logically parallel: "Sleep, gentle heavens, before the prow; / Sleep, gentle winds, as he sleeps now." And the concentration of the lyric's energy inside the stanza is reinforced by indentation, rhyme, and syntax.

> Sphere all your lights around, above;
>> Sleep, gentle heavens, before the prow;
>> Sleep, gentle winds, as he sleeps now,
> My friend, the brother of my love;
>>>> (IX.13–16)

By contrast, the whole energy of the last line is directed forward, while the energy of the first line is directed back. Though each stanza is as taut and self-enclosed as an epitaph inscription, each section is made up of varying numbers of inscriptions, which permit many kinds of internal division.

The hovering and uncertainty of the mourner's bird-like motions match the frequent stalemates in the poem between circular and linear patterns and between forces of closure and delay. In section XII the poet's flight to the southern hemisphere is a lineal breakthrough, literally overriding the break between lines and stanzas at the end of the second quatrain.

> Like her I go; I cannot stay;
>> I leave this mortal ark behind,

> A weight of nerves without a mind,
> And leave the cliffs, and haste away
>
> O'er ocean-mirrors rounded large,
> And reach the glow of southern skies,
>   (XII.5–10)

But circular patterns continue to check the linear movement by showing how the poet's return to England in the last stanza allows the mourner to end where he began. Until then endings are deftly deferred. The first use of the phrase "the end" occurs not at the end of a line but at its middle.

> And saying; 'Comes he thus, my friend?
> Is this the end of all my care?'
> And circle moaning in the air:
> 'Is this the end? Is this the end?'
>   (XII.13–16)

By contrast, when the word recurs two lines later, the first use of "end" does indeed end a question. But it also coincides with a medial caesura. Only the last use of "end," which terminates both a sentence and a quatrain, allows the mention of the word and its use to coincide. Even then the coincidence is incomplete, however, for a glance at the page reveals that the section's closure is postponed for another whole quatrain. Like the betrayal of expectations at the end of *King Lear*, this final surprise prevents the mourner from concluding or resolving anything decisively.

There is so much tranquilizing vagrancy in the elegy—in the re-creation of loved landscapes and in the fond remembering of debates at Cambridge or visits to the Somersby rectory—that the poem's accumulative calmness and humanity appear to bypass all the familiar formulas of elegy. In accepting the mourner's exhaustion and inadequacy, groping blindly toward an anniversary or some other signpost or marker, *In Memoriam* is the opposite of a *tour de force* like "Lycidas." Tennyson cannot bear the thought of life's being ultimately meaningless. But if the dinosaurs that "tare each other in their slime" (56.23) are better adapted to their environment than a species whose life has no meaning after all, the mourner is also prepared to face the fact that a premature death like

Hallam's may be no more tragic metaphysically than the ultimate nothingness we must all come to.

Conscious shaping or straining for effect is written into neither the events of the elegy nor its method. Instead, the elegy becomes a contest for survival from one moment to the next. By inviting us to discern a purgatorial sequence of suffering, like Job's, Tennyson's own label for the poem—"the way of a mourner's soul"—misrepresents the simple stupor and desperation of a mourner who is ready to accept from the beginning almost any distraction or change of plan in thankful relief.

Tennyson's mourner is so stunned and drained of energy, so paralyzed by a sense of comprehensive wrongness, that, unlike most pastoral elegists, he seems not quite up to the task of writing a poem at all. And yet there is a secret freedom in the elegy, a freedom to wander back in time and reach forward, too, that tantalizes the mourner. To exercise this freedom, and yet to think that death may deprive us of it, is for Tennyson the most wrenching part of Hallam's tragedy.

Chapter Four

Staged Versus Real Deaths: Tennyson's Elegies

Nina Auerbach may be right to say that death is the true hero of *Idylls of the King*. It is only when Arthur's cause is lost and the hero is near death, that Guinevere can grasp the value of what she has lost. But one of the profoundest untruths ever voiced about Tennyson also comes from Auerbach, who contends that "with Tennyson as death's laureate, death was never real."[1] That claim would be unintelligible to the mourner in *In Memoriam* or to the poet who wrote the elegiac postscript for Edward Fitzgerald and the verse epistle to Dufferin.

Contrary to what Auerbach says, death is often shockingly real for Tennyson, precisely because he understands so well the scene-stealing theatricality of a death that is merely staged. Death is real in *In Memoriam* because the mourner is too stupefied to understand anything. Not knowing what death means, he refuses to lock himself into any easy comprehension. Hélène Cixous says that writing is "the assault of love on nothingness. . . . The other is safe if I write."[2] Though Tennyson writes *In Memoriam* as a way of "leaving no space for death,"[3] Hallam continues to die in his friend's absence. There is no way of pushing back forgetfulness or of escaping the contradiction of loving completely something he can no longer know or understand.

A composed stage death supports the view that death's touch can be cohering. But even when death is welcomed and anticipated, a stage-tragedy death is often the opposite of consoling. It can hardly be said that, in expressing their longing to die, Tennyson's St. Simeon and Tithonus discover their true selves. It would be more accurate to assert the contrary. Though Tithonus boasts of possessing the dead man's prerogative to forget, it is also a prerogative that is denied him. Often death is attractive only to speakers like Tithonus and Simeon, who are images of living death, unable to achieve real oblivion.

The deaths that are dramatized in Tennyson's juvenilia, in elegiac monologues like "Antony to Cleopatra" and "Mithridates Presenting Berenice with the Cup of Poison," are declamatory stage deaths. Unlike

Shakespeare's Antony, whose death speech releases him into weakness
and allows his official mask to dissolve, Tennyson's Antony sounds
totally in control of his end. Just as the couplets bring each verse to its
foreseen conclusion, so Tennyson's Antony maintains a rigid Roman persona. Though he calls himself "a bleeding Antony" (l.34), we respond to
his death like the audience of a melodrama, whose emotions are felt
deeply but not painfully. We are as comfortably detached from the spectacle of Antony's stage-tragedy death as the audience of the most popular Victorian melodrama, Ellen Wood's *East Lynne*, is detached from the
death of little Willie, who babbles pathetically about the mother he fails
to recognize. If we were not so detached, we would have much less
leisure to grieve over such deaths than we do.

Dragged aloft to his mistress, Shakespeare's Antony has no chance to
view from a distance the slow-motion clumsiness of his botched suicide.
Instead, he is intimately involved in the indignities and embarrassments
that anyone experiences when his body has become a burden to him. His
protracted dying is a part of an everyday world of suffering and humiliation, and like a tired child going to sleep he welcomes whatever comfort
death may bring.

> All length is torture. Since the torch is out,
> Lie down and stray no farther.
> *(Antony and Cleopatra*, IV.xiv.46–49)

By contrast, Tennyson's Antony never allows his Roman mask to slip.
His stage-tragedy death is more in keeping with the calculated dramatic
effects of Shakespeare's Brutus, who speaks as if his whole life has been a
preparation for death.

> So, fare you well at once: for Brutus' tongue
> Hath almost ended his life's history.
> Night hangs upon mine eyes; my bones would rest
> That have but laboured to attain this hour.
> *(Julius Caesar*, V.v.39–42)

Courteous to the "Shades of [his] fathers" (l.39), whose voices he hears
from the tomb, and loyal as ever to his queen, Tennyson's Antony
chooses his last words for maximum dramatic effect. Straining like
Shakespeare's Brutus to make an impact on an audience, he seeks

applause for the way he matches death with his beautifully appropriate response to it.

In Tennyson's *Becket* the martyr prearranges his death to secure maximum tragic effect. He is the producer and director of his own tragedy, and only the shaken Rosamund can elicit in her protests the same blend of foreboding and fear as the chorus of Canterbury women in T. S. Eliot's play *Murder in the Cathedral*. The best way of substituting for the anticipated impact of a stage-tragedy death the tremor of emotion induced by a real-life tragedy is to have the martyrdom presented indirectly through the reaction of some sympathetic observer like Rosamund. This is true even when Rosamund declares by her unawareness of what is happening to the martyr that she is unsuited for the role of an approving observer, which is the part Becket expects her to play. Most incalculable and mysterious is the fact that Becket's martyrdom is performed before an audience that only imperfectly appreciates what he is doing.

In *Queen Mary* Tennyson offers two strikingly discrepant pictures of the queen's death. Elizabeth composes a picture of what Philippe Ariès would call a "beautiful death," in which Mary, acting on Philip's advice, makes Elizabeth her heir. But Elizabeth is her own playwright, writing one kind of death scene for Mary while Tennyson writes another for his audience. Tennyson's picture is one of pure horror, an example of what Ariès calls a "wild" or "untamed" death.[4] Even as Mary's "voice of shipwreck on a shoreless sea" intones its enchanting vowel music, a tremor of emotion is made to pass down her lines. We realize with a shock that, in drawing both knees up to her chin in the posture of an unborn embryo or stiffened corpse, the queen is no longer merely acting out a dramatic part but doing something instinctive, wholly unrehearsed.

Lady Jane's martyrdom in the same play brings a quaver to the voice of her admirer, Bagenhall, whose broken response is as unpremeditated as a spasm. Lacking the leisure to compose in complete sentences, he offers a parataxis of compressed jottings.

> Seventeen—and knew eight languages—in music
> Peerless—her needle perfect, . . .
>
> (III.i, Vol. 8, p. 86)

Though his labored breathing can barely carry him to the end of a line, he manages to linger fondly over his anaphoric triads: "so meek, so modest, / So wife-like humble." As the martyr, like her celebrant, inherits "the great

Silence," even the hangman is left breathless, gasping like Bagenhall in short phrases that exhibit more emotion than the martyr herself.

Cranmer's martyrdom offers an equally interesting case study in the difference between a stage-tragedy death and a real death. At first he seems as zealous for martyrdom as Becket. But in a great soliloquy in Act IV, scene 2, he falters, torn between fears of being a coward and fears of committing sins of arrogance and self-conceit. The tremors of doubt and indecision that mark a genuine truth-seeker who faces real death, not just a stage-tragedy version of it, are easily confused, Cranmer realizes, with the vacillations of a "soft and tremulous coward in the flesh." Are his brain-dazzling colloquies merely numbing, or does self-examination allow Cranmer to anticipate the verdict of history, which may call his deepest beliefs into question?

Cranmer's public confession before his death is both honest and disingenuous. His prayer is sharp and sustained enough to leave no doubt about its personal applicability: "I have offended against heaven and earth / More grievously than any tongue can tell" (IV.iii, vol. 8, p. 151). But his speech is also evasive, because it is generalized enough to prevent his Catholic witnesses from guessing that the sin he repents is the sin of recanting his so-called Protestant heresies. Though the nature of his offense, connivance with his captors, is cunningly withheld until the culminating moment of reversal, Cranmer also seems to be improvising. The truth may come as he is speaking. But until he speaks, he is uncertain how his words will unfold, since he is never sure he will be courageous enough to renounce dissembling or endure more than a stage-tragedy version of a martyr's death. The combination of tenacity and reserve allows Cranmer to save his real meaning for his confession's climax, while winning in the meantime a reputation for contrition and candor.

Near the end of Act II of Tom Stoppard's play *Rosencrantz and Guildenstern are Dead,* Guildenstern protests that "the mechanics of cheap melodrama" is not real death. When an actor performs a death scene on the stage, he screams, chokes, and sinks to his knees, but he "doesn't bring death home to anyone." A real death catches people off-guard and starts "the whisper in their skulls that says—'One day you are going to die.'" The appropriate response to a stage-tragedy death is Lucilia's wrung hands and torn hair in Tennyson's monologue "Lucretius." Comparably melodramatic is the frantic invocation of Simeon to the angels, exhorting them to declare him a saint. Tennyson's Simeon dies in his imagination so many times before his real death, that it is impossible to believe in it.

Conversely, a real death may be theatrically unconvincing. In *Queen Mary* Northumberland's martyrdom so disquiets and unmans him that his death, if presented on stage, would generate far more "sincere" than "significant" emotion. Tennyson wisely reports the death instead of dramatizing it. Stoppard's example of a theatrically unconvincing "real" death is the actor condemned to hang for sheep-stealing, who "did nothing but cry all the time—right out of character—just stood there and cried."[5] By contrast, a good stage-tragedy death requires aesthetic detachment, the kind of dramatic distancing that is notoriously absent in "The Human Cry," the epilogue to "De Profundis," Tennyson's poem on the birth of his son.

One of the most sustained dramatizations of the difference between staged and real deaths comes in the closing moments of the third act of Stoppard's play. Real death, Guildenstern protests to the Player, can never be acted on a stage. There is no applause when someone dies, and no one gets up after it. A dying man's voice trails away and is always lost in the silence. Like a missed heartbeat, real death is a syncope, a suspension of sequence that can be articulated only as a hiatus or a pausing for breath. A real death, properly conceived, is always as understated as the poet's simple failure to reappear one day to the "hoary-headed swain" in Gray's "Elegy." "One morn I missed him on the customed hill" (l.109). Death is "just a man failing to reappear," as Stoppard's Guildenstern says, "that's all—now you see him, now you don't, that's the only thing that's real: here one minute and gone the next and never coming back—an exit, unobtrusive and unannounced, a disappearance gathering weight as it goes on, until, finally, it is heavy with death."[6] Guildenstern acts out the process of real dying in his syntax, which gathers weight through the incremental force of the appositional grammar—"an exit, unobtrusive and unannounced, a disappearance"—and the protracted adverbial clauses that modify the suspended participle, "gathering."

Like Stoppard's Guildenstern, Tennyson's elegists become sympathetic, even intimate with us, whenever they register the shock of death's unexpected caesural breaks and elisions. This is especially true when the shock is so understated, as in the terrible finality of the seeming afterthought—"and he wrote no more"—in the elegiac lines "To the Marquis of Dufferin and Ava" (l.36), that at first we are in danger of missing it. A life seems to expire in the time it takes to pause for breath between the quotation from Lionel's letter and the father's heartbroken comment on it.

A staged death like Arthur's or the Lady of Shalott's makes a strong rhetorical impact. The silent, almost unnoticed passing of Tennyson's son Lionel in the verse epistle to Dufferin induces a strong shock or tremor. As in the lines to Fitzgerald, death intrudes from outside the epistolary convention: it seems harshly at odds with the social convention of writing a letter of thanks to the dead son's hosts in India. One poetic genre has been rudely pushed aside by the uncivil intrusion of another. Indeed the second genre—the elegy—makes the conventions of the first genre void, because it seems to remove all grounds for being thankful. Yeats speaks of the "discourtesy of death" ("In Memory of Major Robert Gregory," l.48). And there is something discourteous about death's intrusion in this poem. Like an uninvited guest, it blunders into a graceful verse epistle, a father's letter of thanks to his son's hosts, where it has no right to be. And yet this unspeakable breach of courtesy is beautifully repaired by Tennyson's own decorum, which gives Lionel's words about the Dufferins' unspeakable kindness to him a heartbreaking turn.

> But ere he left your fatal shore,
> And lay on that funereal boat,
> Dying, 'Unspeakable,' he wrote
> 'Their kindness,' and he wrote no more;
> ("To the Marquis of Dufferin
> and Ava," 11.33–36)

Like his dying son, Tennyson refuses a banal logic of articulating gratitude in favor of a truer and more poignant equivocation: "and he wrote no more." That last clause introduces an elegiac tremor: its indirection and brevity make the death shocking, turning the brevity of a letter into a brevity that is final.

Tennyson, like his son, falters in his capacity to find words. The second-syllable caesura after "Dying" seems to stop the letter-writer in his tracks, almost bringing the poem to a halt. Even the wrenching of word order in the phrase quoted from the son's letter, which is broken apart by the inserted clause "he wrote," seems to break down and sunder Lionel's life. The elegist's voice breaks down, too, as it stops to ponder after the early-breaking caesuras—"Dying," "'Their kindness'"—the enigma of premature endings. The wildness that his lines acquire in touching on the "Unspeakable" loss generates a tremor of emotion that momentarily shatters the urbane tone. Though we are stunned by what Emerson calls "the one wild line out of a private heart," Tennyson barely

touches the subject in passing, so painful is the wound. Forcing himself
to imagine his son's coffin fall and flash in the Red Sea, Tennyson suf-
fuses the lines with what Randall Jarrell calls "the grimness and awful-
ness and untouchable sadness of things."[7]

In a cheerless, dark, and possibly meaningless world, anything
Tennyson can say about his son's death has an air of irrelevance and inadequacy, of awkward silence, which is quite at odds with the urbane self-
possession of the letter-writer, for whom embarrassment is half a sin.
Our response to the magic and repose of Arthur's passing out to sea is
totally at odds with the shock of seeing Lionel pass down into it. We do
not believe in Arthur's stage-tragedy death, and so we have leisure to
grieve over it. But we are shocked by Lionel's death because, as
Tennyson imagines the burial at sea, allowing the unnamable form inside
the coffin to pass forever from the mind's eye, the horror of that distant
event seems unspeakably real. Nothing can mute its shock, because
nothing has quite prepared for it. Caesural breaks make audible the
tremors of pain, the losses that cannot be ritually absorbed and somehow
made less desolating.

Some deaths in Victorian literature are too self-consciously staged to
seem fully real. Even in Tennyson's most staged elegies, however, the
pathos is usually under stricter control than the perfectly genuine but
indulgent pathos in George Eliot's *Amos Barton* or Dickens' *Old Curiosity
Shop*. In Tennyon's "Ulysses," for example, the voyage into death, though
highly ritualized, is not nearly so soothing as the death of Dickens' Paul
Dombey or Little Nell. Ulysses' valedictory rites allow us to feel to the
full the impact of impending doom. But that feeling is controlled by the
heroic mounting of obstacles, which is reinforced by the steady crossing
of the breaks at the end of lines. Even the tone and syntax of Ulysses'
coda send opposite messages. Read in one way, the final phrases drift
down, one by one, with as steady and decisive a conclusion as any poem
can have. But from its beginning, the heroic coda has also been possessed
by the magic of repose, by a tremulous hypnotic rhythm that enchants
and beguiles the speaker. Earlier in the poem Ulysses creates an illusion
of infinite regress by making the margins gleam, fade, and then retreat
from view. The shimmering, mobile words—"Gleams," "fades," and
"move"—impart a tremor of vertigo and add an unsettling evanescence
to the solid arch through which an "untravelled world" is seen racing
away from Ulysses at alarming speed.

Whereas a pastoral elegy will try to rally at the end for an expected
consolation, Tennyson in his elegiac postscript to the monologue

"Tiresias" transgresses this norm by contemplating with a tremor his own imminent death and by wondering aloud, "What life, so maimed by night, were worth / Our living out?" ("To Edward Fitzgerald," ll.79–80). Tiresias' vision of being "gathered to [his] rest" and mingling "with the famous kings of old" ends on an upbeat note ("Tiresias," ll.162–63). For its highly contrived impact the elegiac postscript to Fitzgerald substitutes the tremor of feeling with which a reader contemplates his own death. By speaking, not simply of his own futile march toward the grave, but of "*Our* living out" (l.80) and "*our* poor . . . dawn*" (l.77, my emphases), Tennyson has made Fitzgerald's death our own.

Though Tennyson's anxieties are partly controlled by the conversational ease and urbanity of a verse epistle, his voice quavers with feeling. Tremors are audible in the repetition, three times, of the dread word "night": "past, in sleep, away / By night, into the deeper night! / The deeper night?" ("To Edward Fitzgerald," ll.74–76). These effects are achievements of art, of course. But because they conspire with real and painful experiences that take place outside of art, they leave the impression that the elegist's art has been compromised, interfered with, in some sense marred. Because Tennyson has not had time to reassemble his sense of self, we seem to eavesdrop on his stupor and confusion. Without a chance to put in place any of the elaborate defense mechanisms that associate the dead King Arthur with dignity and purity, Tennyson finds he cannot cheer himself up or allow himself to be eloquent.

Elegies like Tennyson's epistle to Dufferin and Wordsworth's "A Slumber Did My Spirit Seal" confine the dead person to a watery grave or a literal down-to-earth world in which, in contrast to the staged deaths of Arthur or the Lady of Shalott, it is impossible not to believe. Even in "Tithonus" a comparable down-to-earthness keeps coming through the high-flown sentiments, as the literalness of becoming a mere sod or piece of "earth in earth" combines naturally with the ennobling love of the goddess. Some elegies operate in apparent ignorance of the classical conventions. Tennyson's son and Wordsworth's Lucy have not only failed to live through death, like Lycidas, by the aid of the pastoral convention that turns the person mourned into a "genius of the shore." They seem not to be aware of taking part in a rite of passage at all. Oblivious to the "touch of earthly years," both before and after her death, Lucy seems too elemental a force to credit, even by implication, the ritual commemoration that is taking place around her.

Her death is as unpretentious as her spontaneous being as an elemental
creature, almost a nature spirit, not quite human, but not wholly natural
either. Like Lucy's sudden removal, Lionel's death strikes the mourner
dumb. But there is no suggestion that the forces that operate in nature
have contrived that this is so. It just happens, like the unforeseeable
event that creates a break between the two quatrains of "A Slumber Did
My Spirit Seal," even though there seems at first to be no discernible
change in either subject matter or tone. So, too, in Tennyson's verse epistle, the change death brings seems at first so minimal—"and he wrote
no more" (l.36)—that we are in danger of missing it. It is the unawareness of Lionel or Lucy, the total unconsciousness of being tragic or
pathetic, that makes each death painful.

The boldest intimation of immortality in Tennyson's elegies, section
95 of *In Memoriam*, is accompanied by an odd increment of energy.
Though there is something stagy about the rocking of the full-foliaged
elms and flowers by the gathering breeze, what happens after the talking breeze subsides is the opposite of theatrical. The breeze announces,

> "The dawn, the dawn," and died away;
>   And East and West, without a breath,
>   Mixt their dim lights, like life and death,
> To broaden into boundless day.
>   (*In Memoriam*, 95.61–64)

When "seen at the right angle," as Stoppard's player would say, there
unexpectedly escapes from this merging of the afterglow of sunset with
the first glimmer of dawn on midsummer nights a blending of forms
that momentarily cracks "the shell of mortality."[8] And yet so unobtrusively does the mourner introduce his prophecy about dying into life,
and so quietly and undemonstratively does he bind the simile in which it
appears to the rest of the quatrain, that tenor and vehicle have already
reversed themselves before we register the impact of this most spectacular yet least theatrical transformation in the poem.

The Talmud says that "a word is worth one coin; silence is worth
two."[9] Because death, like the heart, is the great ellipsis that teaches with
silence and speaks through silence, Tennyson knows that an elegist can
say most when he speaks least. As he shows in his best elegies, death is

mute and invisible, and takes place in the blanks created by dashes, caesural breaks, and surgical slashes of ellipsis and omission. The stage-tragedy triumphs of Tennyson's Antony, St. Simeon, Tithonus, Ulysses, and even Lucretius, come at the penultimate moment. The ultimate moment itself cannot be dramatized.

Chapter Five

A Genre Under Siege:
Idylls of the King

In a traditional epic the interpreter's job is to assign praise or blame to a hero like Arthur or an antihero like Lancelot for particular actions he performs. As Yeats says of *The Faerie Queene*, Spenser "wrote of knights and ladies, wild creatures imagined by the aristocratic poets of the twelfth century . . . , but he fastened them with allegorical nails to a big barn-door of common sense, of merely practical virtue."[1] In *Idylls of the King* Tennyson's moral understanding is the direct opposite of Spenser's. He wants to be as just and impartial as Spenser, but to that end he wants to feel acutely every kind of partiality: the adulterous love of Lancelot and Guinevere no less than Arthur's virtue. Though truth is a mystery, not a delusion, Tennyson believes that everyone in a dispute is to some degree right. Because the greatest lies about Arthur or Guinevere, and the greatest truths, may be found side by side, he refuses to give a halo to Arthur and a halter to Guinevere. He does something more interesting: he gives both of them voices.

Tennyson's idylls disturb and transform the conventions of epic and Arthurian poetry by *not* permitting decisions on moral questions, but by making us see the sanctions and motives on all sides. Two contradictory scales of value—the practical scale of Arthur and the visionary one of Galahad—are unequivocally stated. But there is no attempt or desire to qualify one by the other or to decide which (if either) is right. Tennyson uses his moral intelligence to see all around a complex issue, not to make decisive judgments.

When Arthur finally arrives at Leodogran's castle in "The Coming of Arthur," his future queen fails to notice him, even though he stands out from all the other knights because his face is bare. The reader's uneasy sense of being unexpectedly and slightly out of step with the norms of conventional romance and heroic narrative is repeated regularly in *Idylls of the King*. The first facts a reader expects to learn about King Arthur are his origins, his marriage, and how he came to unite his kingdom. But on all three counts the reader's expectations are temporarily betrayed.

By focusing on Arthur's military quest, Tennyson leads us to assume that Arthur establishes his kingship by military means. But Arthur has to overcome an opposition to his rule that is psychological and moral rather than military: uncertainty about his origins. No sooner, however, have we adjusted our expectations to accord with a threat to Arthur's rule that is epistemological and vaguely metaphysical in nature (who is Arthur, this "Ideal manhood closed in real man," and how can we know?), than the brutal hacking and assault of warrior kings restore the military action we thought we had left behind:

> they swerved and brake
> Flying, and Arthur called to stay the brands
> That hacked among the flyers.
> ("The Coming of Arthur," ll.118–20)

As we follow, our minds are in constant but quiet flux, always shifting among questions of origin, marriage, and kingship, without ever completely leaving familiar ground. Tennyson transforms the conventions of epic poetry and romance by refusing to cradle the mind in a closed framework. Instead, he allows us to comprehend—and hold onto—all the contradictions the poem contains. Continually slipping in and out of different frames of reference, *Idylls of the King* is bigger than any single genre or any single set of epic conventions we have for knowing it.

The reader's uncertainty about Arthur's origins continues in "Gareth and Lynette." If the seer can see through Gareth's outward appearance, why is Arthur himself not able to penetrate the "young lad's mystery"? Does Arthur have less insight than his seer? Gareth's disclosure of his identity solves one problem, but by the time the difficulty of making him faithful to both Bellicent and Arthur is met, the reader has encountered new problems. Gareth's fidelity to his mother cannot be construed as a deception of Arthur without compromising Gareth, but in saving Gareth does Tennyson not compromise Arthur? Readers do not so much shift their focus as find it shifted for them. We are no longer concerned about Gareth's deceptions but about other people's ability to penetrate his masks. Our mind becomes one with the baron's, whose query whether Lynette "be mad, or else the King, / Or both or neither" (ll.854–55) echoes the earlier confusions of the seer. The poem disturbs its genre by keeping our minds in a constant state of motion between "Confusion, and illusion, and relation"(l.281). This motion is appropriate, not only to paradoxes and evasions (or even to poems about paradoxes and evasions), but also to the actual experience of paradox and evasion itself.

"The Marriage of Geraint" and "Geraint and Enid" bring a succession of both expected and unexpected reversals. The pattern is established in miniature in Enid's song, which traces the turn of the "wild wheel through sunshine, storm, and cloud" (1.348). In "The Marriage of Geraint" the hero begins in acknowledged ignorance; he does not even know his adversary's name. Though Geraint is just as ignorant in "Geraint and Enid," he is dangerously unaware of his ignorance. The earlier idyll makes the reader perceive adversity and fortune simultaneously. We are made to feel the dependence of one upon the other: a pattern of coherence in incoherence. The later idyll disturbs this pattern by making us think of order and disorder successively.

Geraint embodies the principle of order and authority lacking in the anarchy of the preceding idyll. But his rigid antitheses, though smoothed by alliteration and syntactical balance, make him harsh and ill-tempered.

> 'Did I wish
> Your warning or your silence? one command
> I laid upon you, not to speak to me,
> And thus you keep it! Well then, look—for now,
> Whether ye wish me victory or defeat,
> Long for my life, or hunger for my death,
> Yourself shall see my vigour is not lost.'
> ("Geraint and Enid," ll.76–82)

The later violence of Earl Doorm, who poses a threat to coherence, is at first satisfying to a reader who feels uneasy at Geraint's own abuse of order. But the orderliness that the reader values in Geraint's victory over Edyrn is momentarily disturbed by new manifestations of disorder. *Idylls of the King* persists in this disturbance of norms. It introduces false conceptions of order. Then in destroying these unsatisfying conceptions it brings us to the verge of chaos, eventually using a near-miraculous reversal of events—"So died Earl Doorm by him he counted dead" ("Geraint and Enid," l.729)—to restore a new, more complex sense of simultaneous order *and* disorder. The constant pull of opposites resembles the contending forces of identity and difference that are always at war in any strong use of metaphor.

In "Balin and Balan" and "Pelleas and Ettarre" the mind is a place to be avoided, because of what is present there. Guinevere's adultery and Pelleas' betrayal by Gawain, who is seduced by the woman he has promised to woo for his friend, are unacknowledged or concealed. Cynics like Tristram and Gawain assume that loathsome things go on in the mind which most people prefer not to talk about and yet cannot prevent happening.

If Guinevere is the villain of the piece, why has Tennyson disturbed the norms of epic narrative by making her attractive? Tennyson wants to show that, like most tragic heroines, she is unsuited for her role as adulteress and deceiver. The directness and simplicity of everything she says about her love for Lancelot are compromised by the lies and concealment that prevent her being what she is by nature: a spontaneously open woman. Ironically, the ingenuous heroine finds something she cannot be open about, while the close man, Arthur, who is too reticent and unworldly to be an effective ruler, finds it possible to dramatize himself as candid and engaging—too good for this world perhaps, but still a model of tact and forgiveness. What conspires against Arthur are the roles that are thrust upon him, epic roles for which he is unsuited, and which subtly but decisively separate him from the world of intrigue and deceit he has to live in.

Lancelot's generosity and openness, qualities Guinevere loves in him, are driven underground and gradually destroyed. Conversely, the natural reserve and even deviousness of Arthur, who may suspect his wife's adultery from the beginning—and even drive her to it—allow him to be seen as the opposite of devious. As the popular and open Lancelot and Guinevere are immobilized, the aloof and private Arthur is free to play the role of sympathetic scapegoat: the victim to whom the transfer of guilt imparts the dignity of innocence. Challenging the norms of Arthurian epic, these tricky reversals of candor and deviousness poison the atmosphere without in any way diminishing our intimacy with Arthur and his queen.

Apart from their adultery, everything about Lancelot's and Guinevere's lives seems innocent and normal. Lancelot has no knowledge of Elaine's love for him, and his passion for the Queen is no sudden infatuation but a love that is enduring and committed. Like *Paradise Lost*, a Victorian melodrama would have cast Lancelot and Guinvere as the villains of the piece. But Tennyson's Lancelot is not Satan, nor is Guinevere Eve.

It is both strange and natural that Guinevere should silently protect and defend Arthur without doing anything to diminish or renounce her love for Lancelot. Arthur's forgiveness of Guinevere brings husband and wife close together in a way that no conspiracy against Lancelot or no resolve to be avenged on Guinevere could have done. The most moving thing about the forgiveness scene is how Guinevere's anguished response dies away in a renewal of her vows to Arthur, even though her husband does not stay to hear them. In spite of all Arthur's words of mingled forgiveness and reproach, and her own feelings of betrayal, Guinevere's marriage vows are not overturned. They are kept intact (most unexpectedly) by her love for Lancelot, and by the surprising dignity with which she also renews her commitment to Arthur. He is the husband she has always craved to love—and in some ways continues to love—more than Lancelot:

> It would have been my pleasure had I seen.
> We needs most love the highest when we see it,
> Not Lancelot, nor another.
>
> ("Guinevere," ll.654–56)

We are made to feel Guinevere's happiness with Lancelot, despite the bitterness it brings her in this scene. But we are also made to see that she should not have sacrificed the equally intimate pleasures she could have shared with Arthur. The simple moralist wants to conclude that all is black and white. But Tennyson knows the world is deeply ambiguous and that acceptance of these ambiguities is at the center of regeneration.

Tennyson disturbs and transforms the absolutes of epic narrative by recognizing the claims of people who are human and weak and who have to live, as Arthur cannot, in morally ambiguous situations. Unlike the deranged Balin or the crazed Pelleas, Lancelot and Guinevere are neither fanatics nor psychopaths: they are lovers who acquire their own dignity and strength. Though everything Lancelot does in *Idylls of the King* is disingenuous, his words and deeds still reveal that he would like to be virtuous if he could. Like Merlin, Vivien's discerning victim, Lancelot makes us intimate with a compulsion to be seduced and enslaved that is all too compatible with clearsightedness. He understands how ordinary morality depends on flesh-and-blood people like himself. His tolerance for the very weaknesses that impair morality is one of the reasons Guinevere cares for Lancelot and why it is as easy for her to fall in love with him as it is for her to breathe.

For comparable confusions of moral and aesthetic values in Arthurian poetry we have only to turn to William Morris's poem, "The Defence of Guenevere," where slippages are captured in a series of lovely "cadences" or falls.

> as if one should
>
> Slip slowly down some path worn smooth and even,
> Down to a cool sea on a summer day;
> Yet still in slipping was there some small leaven
>
> Of stretched hands catching small stones by the way . . .
>
> No minute of that wild day ever slips
>
> From out my memory
>
> (ll.93–106)

The moral slippage of the word "slip" is beautifully disguised as a refreshing slip down a seaside path on a summer day and then as slipping that is the opposite of slippage, since it binds the event to memory with gratitude and affection. Such repetitions of a word are valued, not for their meaning, which is hollowed out by casuistry and special pleading, but for their enigmatic formal qualities, like a refrain in a ballad or a recurrent cadence in a song, whose "fall"—both moral and musical—resonates more seductively each time it is heard.

In "Balin and Balan" the world will no longer support the civilizing standards represented for Balin by Guinevere's emblem, the crown-royal. Though the impossibility of Balin's task of choosing, establishing, and maintaining the value of these standards makes the very effort seem wayward or vagrant, Tennyson himself disturbs the norms of the conventional satire on madness by reminding us that the maintenance of values is one of the most necessary and sane activities of any human mind.

In a story devoted to the education of an idealist, one of two scenarios usually unfolds. Either the threats to the hero's idealism are shown to be

illusory and hence easily overcome, as in the case of Gareth's and
Geraint's antagonists; or else the threats are real, like Ettarre's, but still
educative in bringing the idealist to a less naive understanding of himself
and the world. By contrast, "Balin and Balan" disturbs and transforms
its genre by disallowing the reader the intellectual comfort of being con-
fined to a system of values that discounts Vivien's testimony. Though we
discredit Vivien as a liar, we know that her supposed falsehood about
Guinevere, whose love for Lancelot seems good in itself, is not the lie it
seems to be. There is nothing in "Balin and Balan" to keep the reader
safe from confusion, comfortably outside the action, sharing secrets with
Tennyson behind his characters' backs.

The idyll is not simply the ironic story of two brothers who are confused and self-deceived. It is also the story of the reader's own confusions. As in "Lancelot and Elaine," where Lancelot's "faith unfaithful"
keeps him "falsely true" (l.872), we are asked to consider Balin's devotion to an ideal in too many of the bewildering frames that are usually
available to readers only outside the comfortable limitations of art. For
example, Balin's devotion to the queen is presented variously as the sal-
vation of a prodigal son, a religion, a self-deception, a willful refusal to
accept the evidence of his senses, a heel of Achilles, and even a form of
fanaticism and mental illness. As we move from one frame of evaluation
to another with a rapidity that matches Balin's own wayward zeal, our
misplaced faith in the constancy of any single frame begins to make the
whole enterprise look foolish.

The more proof Balin has of Guinevere's infidelity, the more desper-
ately he affirms her innocence. His mind has walked into a trap, and the
idyll both invites us inside that trap and warns us to stay out.

> Queen? subject? but I see not what I see.
> Damsel and lover? hear not what I hear.
>   ("Balin and Balan," ll.276–77)

We are close to Balin, wanting to believe what he believes, and yet alienated from his own refusals to understand. When Garlon insults Balin for
wearing Guinevere's emblem, which he calls the "crown-scandalous"
(l.384), a strain between comic and tragic treatments can suddenly be
felt. Balin continues to exalt Guinevere's story as a love tragedy, while
Garlon mocks it in terms of a different genre altogether: the comedy of
sexual intrigue.

"Pelleas and Ettarre" reveals that cynicism and sentiment are closely connected. The sentiment of love that lends "All the young beauty of [Pelleas's] . . . soul" (l.79) to the harlot Ettarre is a form of self-love. His later cynicism and sexual loathing, when he lays his naked sword across the throats of his false friend, Gawain, and the promiscuous Ettarre, expresses his humiliated sense of how he, the sexual innocent, must look to a detached onlooker, and how the behavior of dupes often looks to him. Most disquieting is the sexual loathing Pelleas feels as he crushes "the saddle with his thighs," clenches "His hands," and maddens himself with moans (ll.450–51). Like Balin, Pelleas has been trying to assimilate comedy to tragedy, sex to love. But neither is able to protect the fragile idealism of courtly love against the bitter comedy of sexual scandal and intrigue. Each remains locked in the vise of his own separate obsessions.

> The beauty of her flesh abashed the boy,
> As though it were the beauty of her soul:
> ("Pelleas and Ettarre," ll.74–75)

Pelleas the courtly lover has been exalting love while Ettarre has been peddling sex. There is no way we can inhabit the idealist's mind—with its imagination of romance and innocence—at the same time we are trapped inside the agonizing mind of the sexual dupe and cynic. Nowhere are the *Idylls* more Victorian than in their sense that a love poem is an ennobling genre of adventure and romance, whereas sex belongs to a genre of black comedy, a poetry of scandal and intrigue.

Tennyson disturbs and transforms the conventions of the moral tale, not by denying but by broadening and intensifying our kinship with Pelleas, even when Pelleas himself is bestialized and degraded. In the moral deformity of Pelleas' longing to forget he is a man by coupling with wolves we are invited to contemplate a terrible potentiality of all thwarted longing and desire.

For Guinevere and Lancelot themselves, however, the distinction between the lover and the connoisseur of sex ceases to apply. Guinevere's physical intimacy with Lancelot is expressed with as much directness as is compatible with female dignity. And yet her tender statement of what she loves and admires in Lancelot, the bounty of his mind and his generous heart, far exceeds mere sexual satisfaction. Though there is one beauty of the body and another of the "noble mind," we are made to feel

that in the end both are united in a single harmony where each fulfills
and dignifies the other.

The breadth and generosity of Tennyson's mind are nowhere more
evident than in the balanced praise Guinevere accords the "loyal nature"
and "noble mind" of both Lancelot and Arthur.

> 'Sir Lancelot, as became a noble knight,
> Was gracious to all ladies, and the same
> In open battle or the tilting-field
> Forebore his own advantage, and the King
> In open battle or the tilting-field
> Forebore his own advantage, and these two
> Were the most nobly-mannered men of all;
> For manners are not idle, but the fruit
> Of loyal nature, and of noble mind.'
>
> ("Guinevere," ll.326–34)

The intelligence and poise of this tribute bring out capacities of confidence, nobility, and courtesy to women, which also enforce our sense of
human frailty in Guinevere and Lancelot. Two perspectives are clearly
apprehended and kept in balance by the parallel syntax and anaphora—
"In open battle," "Forebore his own advantage," "In open battle,"
"Forebore his own advantage"—which repeat without change the
"nobly-mannered" behavior of both men.

Tennyson disturbs the conventions of visionary poetry by turning the
most visionary idyll, "The Holy Grail," into a poem more concerned to
veil a vision than reveal it. Instead of focusing transparently on the
visionary Galahad, the idyll uses a narrator, Percivale, to distance what is
seen. As human filters are made to intervene between the visionary
imagination and its object, the idyll becomes a story about the puzzling
relation of a teller to his tale. If the Holy Grail were seen steadily and
whole, it would be perceived only as an object in time and space. But
because Percivale has only a fugitive and vanishing glimpse of the Grail,
he possesses it as a norm of vision that oversees what he sees. In
Northrop Frye's words, the Grail "is not an object, but something uniting the objective [world] with ourselves."[2]

In "The Last Tournament," the spectacular low point of the *Idylls*, the
demoralization brought about by Tristram's and Isolt's breaking of their

vows creates an instant kind of bankruptcy. The decay is captured in the decadent ethic of Tristram's song, which is giddy in its display of weightless emotional vigor and its dazzling turns upon a few repeated words.

> New leaf, new life—the days of frost are o'er:
> New life, new love, to suit the newer day:
> New loves are sweet as those that went before:
> Free love—free field—we love but while we may.
> ("The Last Tournament," ll.278–81)

Like the fool Dagonet, Tristram turns verbal cartwheels, beguiled as much by the alliterating sound of his words as by their meaning. In decomposing the unity of language to give a separate excitement or thrill to each individual phrase and word, his rhetoric proves at least as decadent as the hollowed-out rituals of the Tournament of the Dead Innocence.

The absence of any inward certitude or belief is deftly captured in the quick but squalid fade-out which extinguishes Tristram's lust as if it were a flame flickering for an instant in the dark.

> Out of the dark, just as the lips had touched,
> Behind him rose a shadow and a shriek—
> 'Mark's way,' said Mark, and clove him through the brain.
> ("The Last Tournament," ll.746–48)

Dagonet's songs are jovially exuberant. But like Thersites' jests in *Troilus and Cressida*, they are also strident and jeering. Reducing everything to his own level, the Fool has no weapon but his tongue. Even his language is lethal, and feeds on itself as greedily as the ever-present lechery and lust.

> and the wan day
> Went glooming down in wet and weariness:
> ("The Last Tournament," ll.214–15)

> I have wallowed, I have washed—the world
> Is flesh and shadow—I have had my day.

> The dirty nurse, Experience, in her kind
> Hath fouled me—an I wallowed, then I washed—
>> ("The Last Tournament," ll.315–18)

Words in love with their own sound assume a mercenary, venal quality, whether at the service of Tennyson's narrator or the Fool.

The death of language is comparable to the lethal operations Morris performs on words in "King Arthur's Tomb." As Christopher Ricks observes in *Beckett's Dying Words*, language becomes deathlike when it acquires the power to mean its own opposite.[3]

> Why did your long lips cleave
> In such strange way unto my fingers then?
> So eagerly glad to kiss, so loath to leave
> When you rose up?
>> ("King Arthur's Tomb," ll.249–52)

There is a lethal aliveness in the verb "cleave," which can mean "cut asunder" as well as "cling to." Usually, words are tipped with arrows: when Tennyson's Ancient Sage exhorts the skeptic to "cleave . . . to the sunnier side of doubt" (l.68), he uses "cleave" to point in one direction only. But Morris gives us the axis without the arrow: even as Arthur's "long lips" "cleave . . . unto" the fingers, they also seem to "cleave . . . in two," mutilating what they kiss. We catch the flicker of an "anti-pun" in the archaic preposition "unto," which is no longer alive on any speaker's tongue. The phantom meaning of *in two*, which is mordantly alive in the preposition *unto*, cannot be wholly banished from the mind once it is raised. As in dreams, where there are no contraries, the paralyzing possibility that Arthur's lips are long because they tarry long, to immobilize and kill as well as kiss and restore to life, makes the language deathlike. We feel what Ricks calls "the torpedo-touch"[4] in "cleave," whose antithetical senses give the kiss a sinister glow. Like Tennyson's Maud, whose ghastly glimmer has the luminous appearance of a ghost, Lancelot, for all his ardor and lust, has the emotional vigor of a vampire.

When Tennyson's Isolt insists that Tristram swear to love her "even when [she is] old, / Gray-haired, and past desire" (ll.647–48), his refusal to make vows has its own profane cogency. Since vows are only "the wholesome madness of an hour" (l.670), hollowed out by time, which wrings the quality and faith out of everything, they exhibit Arthur's solemn and high-minded kind of folly, a distemper that "the wide world" merely scorns (l.690). Isolt's sad, teasing sense that everything slips away into a void and that Tristram's vow to be faithful to her will never be sworn resembles in its wry pursuit of phantoms one of Tristram's own bitter songs: "Free love—free field—we love but while we may" (l.275).

The piercing penetration of little Dagonet, who pronounces Arthur "king of fools" (l.354) for thinking he can make figs out of thistles, gives him the soundest judgment in the idyll. But the comedy of the wise fool, dancing without a roundelay to dance to, is a form of "eating dry," as Tristram says (l.249), that places the giddy moment of fun in a world of nightmare. Like the fool's vigorous dancing, and Isolt's spur-of-the-moment appeal to Tristram to desire her even when she is past desiring, the dislocated energy makes everything seem aimless. The whirl of events suspends the revelers over voids of inner madness.

Even when the epic similes produce flickers of gratuitous beauty, the narrative has difficulty digesting them. The simile of the mountain in midsummer snows, for example, when all the purple slopes of flowers "Pass under white, till the warm hour returns" (l.230), does nothing to dignify the tawdry revels. The similes tend to work the other way round, producing incongruity of effect. The great waves breaking upon the coast, "Whitening for half a league," and then thinning themselves "Far over sands marbled with moon and cloud, / From less and less to nothing," are beautifully evoked (ll.464–66). But since Tennyson uses the waves to describe something ugly and bathetic, the heavy-headed fall of a drunken knight, the irrelevant splendor seems merely decadent. One sign of this decadence is Tennyson's habit of decomposing his verse to give special prominence to the similes, and of decomposing the similes to give place to the sound pattern or the resonance of an individual word.

Though Isolt flirts with Tristram and seduces him, she is also the opposite of coy. Surprisingly, as she pours out the depth of her desire for Tristram: "My God, the measure of my hate for Mark / Is as the measure of my love for thee" (ll.535–36), she sounds more wistful than cynical and more tender- than tough-minded.

> I had forgotten all in my strong joy
> To see thee—yearnings?—ay! for, hour by hour,
> Here in the never-ended afternoon,
> O sweeter than all memories of thee,
> Deeper than any yearnings after thee

> Seemed those far-rolling, westward-smiling seas,
> Watched from this tower.
>
> ("The Last Tournament," ll.578–84)

In one sense, the seductive starts and hesitations of her rhetoric are not to be trusted. Yet in another sense they are wholly true to what she feels. Two levels are operating: the hidden level of calculation and will, and the spontaneously open assertion of a deep longing and homesickness for the man she loves.

What is most contrived about Isolt's longing is also most affecting. She knows that like the whirling Dagonet, time dances so fast and giddily that it seems to stand still, frozen in the frame of a fleeting present. But she grieves, and wishes it were otherwise. If everything exists in a specious present, as Tristram says, then their vows abolish themselves in the act of being spoken. Isolt is sick at heart when she realizes that her love has no saving growth or future prospects. Since her life is consumed in chasing phantoms, it is wasted with a special distemper of the spirit: there is something ill about her heart that will never heal.

At the beginning of the idyll Dagonet is still in control, using his witty home truths to welcome Arthur as a "brother fool," "the king of fools" (ll.352, 358). But after Mark murders Tristram and the ceremony of innocence is drowned, the Fool's stage disappears from under him.

> about his feet
> A voice clung sobbing till he questioned it,
> 'What art thou?' and the voice about his feet
> Sent up an answer, sobbing, 'I am thy fool,
> And I shall never make thee smile again.'
>
> ("The Last Tournament," ll.752–56)

Unable to play his part upon the court stage, Dagonet is pushed out into the "death-dumb autumn-dripping gloom" (l.750), where he sets up an oddly reproachful wail, like a waif. Failing to rise to the crisis, the Fool can only concede the irrelevance and total inadequacy of his art.

For a poet who proclaims the importance of duty and conscience, "the royal in thyself" ("To the Queen," l.1), Tennyson is as notoriously ambiguous about the meaning of duty as his disillusioned fool, Dagonet. Though the knights have an obligation to imitate Arthur by working hard in their allotted field, in "The Holy Grail" they also have a duty to chase visionary rainbows like Galahad, even when these rainbows burst like bubbles in their hands. Presumably Guinevere has a duty to be faithful to Arthur. But is susceptibility to Lancelot's courtesy and poise, to his great nobility of mind, not a duty, too? The only way we can understand Gareth's marriage to Lynette or Geraint's to Enid as a form of "duty" is to say that they have a duty to their own happiness. Though Lancelot also feels a duty to his happiness, it is an immediate cause of Camelot's ruin.

We miss the point of *Idylls of the King* if we fail to see that one of its targets is the moral authority of Tennyson himself. The poet is less entranced by the solemn thunder-rolls of Merlin's prophecies than by the enchantments of sound that disjoin Guinevere's beautiful sensations of Lancelot's "loyal nature" and "noble mind" form a reader's judgment or understanding of them. Perhaps it is only Tennyson's sympathy for a reader's desire for coherence that prevents his glorying in art's reduced moral ambition and freedom from vatic utterance or cant. As it is, Tennyson's moral discriminations are so fine and his sympathies so subtle that we begin to suspect there is no wickedness like Guinevere's in which he could not discover some virtue, and no blamelessness like Arthur's in which he could not discover some deep failing or fault. His epic poem disturbs and transforms the conventions of moral allegory by trying to make morality consistent with uncertainty. Only about uncertainty itself is he certain.[5]

PART TWO
A Ventriloquized World

Douglas Bush observes that in Yeats, T. S. Eliot, and Frost "we hear somewhat varied intonations of one always recognizable voice." Tennyson, by contrast, "is a ventriloquist, or a troupe of ventriloquists."[1] The second part of this monograph tests Bush's metaphor by asking two questions: Are such diverse poems as Tennyson's "St. Simeon Stylites" and "Locksley Hall," *Maud* and "Ulysses" the impersonations of a single ventriloquist, or of a whole corps of them? And how far can a poet of negative capability impersonate a host of human or nonhuman subjects without losing his own distinctive identity and voice?

Both questions are implicit in the argument of W. J. Fox, one of Tennyson's earliest reviewers, who describes the poet as a "transmigrating Vishnu."[2] Incarnating himself as a fabulous sea monster as readily as a mermaid or a forsaken woman, Tennyson displays the powers of the Hindu god Vishnu, who assumes the most abased and lofty forms. By seeing more clearly Tennyson's limitations as a playwright, we should also better appreciate the genius of his dramatic monologues and his monodrama, *Maud*, which combine the seer's talent for hearing voices with the ventriloquist's gift for projecting them.

Chapter Six

The Trespass of Intimacy: Tennyson's Closeness to Speakers Unsuited for their Roles

Tennyson's best dramatic monologues are sustained exercises in what W. H. Empson calls "double irony," the simultaneous endorsement of contradictory codes.[1] Because the speakers in such monologues are pulled two ways at once, their incapacity to pursue wholeheartedly any single course of action unsuits them for their roles. Far from alienating us, however, the indecision and vulnerability that are characteristic of these speakers make us surprisingly intimate with them.

The Lotos-eaters, for example, urge a life of pastoral leisure and ease. But they are too passionately in love with life to mistake lotos for hashish, or to confuse the allure of a recreative paradise like Spenser's garden of Adonis with the merely drugged existence of Swinburne's garden of Proserpine. Like apprentice advocates, the Lotos-eaters must use the stagy pathos of their ever climbing up the climbing wave to convince Ulysses, an unsympathetic censor, that their choice of lotos-land is worthy of them. And Ulysses must spend much of his monologue in a mock debate with Telemachus. He must defend in the most stirring possible terms his controversial decision to leave Ithaca to follow knowledge like a sinking star. Tennyson's Ulysses is a mirror image of the Lotos-eaters: he embraces heroic values. But even in celebrating "One equal temper of heroic hearts" (l.68) he is beguiled by a round-and-round hypnotic movement that enchants and beguiles him. He is already half in love with easeful death.

By intellectual persuasion Tennyson's Lucretius is an atheist and materialist. But by temperament he is hopelessly unsuited for that role, celebrating the grandeur of his universe even as he exposes its absurdities. As John Keble grasped, Lucretius' imagination is all on the side of the religion that his intellect rejects. Though he might accept religion in Santayana's sense, as "the poetry of truth," like Plato he seems (in Philip

Sidney's phrase) to have "defile[d] the Fountaine out of which his [own] flowing streames have proceeded."[2]

Like Maud's lover, Tennyson's Lucretius discovers during his mental breakdown that consciousness can be as wide and sweeping as the flaring atom streams of his materialist cosmology. But if the mind has a material composition, its spacious wanderings are an anomaly, as unforeseen and irrelevant as his wife's mistaken notions of moral obligation: "Care not thou! / Thy duty? What is duty? Fare thee well!" ("Lucretius," ll.279–80).

Ironically, the loving Lucilia is quite unsuited for the drama in which her dying husband tries to cast her. Because she loves Lucretius and is touched when he bares his inmost feelings to her, she is also appalled by what her love philter has done to his manhood. Her love and his heightened sensuality, as well as the newfound intimacy between them, unfit both characters for the roles they are called upon to play.

We become intimate with Lucretius when he lets his defenses down and reveals truths about his repressed affective life. Since erotic fantasies of shameless oreads and satyrs are damaging to Lucretius' reputation as a dispassionate philosopher, he has taken elaborate precautions to hide these sensual impulses, even from himself. In beating her breast and tearing her hair for helping Lucretius dispatch himself to a "Passionless bride" of "divine Tranquillity," "Without one pleasure and without one pain" (ll.265, 268), Lucilia is clearly more unhinged and distraught than the dying philosopher she hoped to make more amorous.

It is because she loves her husband that Lucilia is destroyed by him, crying "out upon herself / As having failed in duty to him" ("Lucretius," ll.276–77). The intimacy she professes to find lacking in Lucretius, who reserves his passion (not for mistresses) but for his Muse, is also a quality she can love in him, once she understands its motives. But just when an understanding of these motives has begun to draw Lucilia back to her husband, supplying the kind of free intimacy that was lacking in their marriage, Lucretius terminates all such intimacies forever by driving a knife through his side. Our closeness to Lucretius comes from a sense that a philosopher so sublime in his conceptions and so eloquent in his language is temperamentally unsuited to the reductive tasks an atheist and materialist must set himself.

Even at the heart of death, speakers in Tennyson's monologues continue to exercise a whimsical freedom over it. We know Lucretius is too fine an orator to commit suicide before he has finished his great speech. Though his death is administered by too strong a love philter, it is postponed until Lucretius takes matters into his own hands by vanquishing a Roman by a Roman.

A mask often slips when a disenchanted or exhausted speaker manages to relax. In the confessional "twilight" mood of Browning's Andrea del Sarto, who says he has "grown peaceful as old age," "regret[s] little," and "would change still less" (ll.244–45), Tennyson's Tithonus is quite ready to substitute for his "cruel immortality" a one-way trip of dust to dust. Though the "earth in earth" he seeks movingly contrasts with the circular return, "morn by morn," of the goddess (ll.74–75), his lingering shade also shows that death is both easy and difficult: it is everywhere, but unless we commit suicide it eludes us at the exact moment we reach out to touch it.

Tithonus's earlier version of himself as an immortal youth, the consort of Aurora, produces a momentary illusion of sensuous immediacy combined with permanence. The exuberant ardor of his conceit that the goddess's "cheek begins to redden through the gloom," and that her "sweet eyes brighten slowly close to" his ("Tithonus," ll.37–38), touches us with its irreducible simplicity and tenderness. Incongruously, however, this most sensitive of speakers, an aesthete afflicted with a panic-stricken sense of the transience and hence the seriousness of beauty, aspires to a totally insensate state, the enduring grimness of "Immortal age" (l.22).

Tithonus's big scene fails because he has cast himself for a role in an Ovidian love story in which his partner, the beautiful Aurora, cannot participate. Her indulgent smile is not a dramatic trick, but the natural response of someone who seems to have wandered into the monologue from a different genre, and who, as the advent of day, is not a conventional dramatic character at all. Tithonus cannot understand an auditor whose silence, lack of artifice, and ignorance of role-playing threaten his whole dramatic conception of himself as a deceived lover. From his disenchanted perception of his beloved's cruel oxymorons, her emotionless tears and cold rosy shadows, Tithonus can only turn back into nature, to die there—if he can.

Though Tithonus yearns for passion and awareness that transcend time, he is also so deeply in love with sensuous immediacy that he is ready to forsake his avowed goal in order to make the sensory world more lovely. Like Demeter, he shows that though mortality is a misfortune, so is its opposite. These speakers' two-way meanings and free intimacies of consciousness are perhaps the most enduring and appealing quality of their great monologues.

Our intimacy with speakers who let their masks drop in a casual aside is based on a special and open relation with gesture and intonation. Though inadvertent disclosures are usually better suited to a soliloquy or monologue than to a stage play, some scenes in Tennyson's historical drama, *Becket,* are a striking exception. Though the politics of state requires King Henry to be a stern censor of a friend turned enemy, this is not what his language of intimacy reveals him to be.

> Co-mates we were, and had our sport together,
> Co-kings we were, and made the laws together.
> (II, ii, Vol. 9, p. 105)

Parities of syntax bind the verses, as they bind the friends, with words that recur without variation at the head and end of successive lines. The repeating elements are as constant as the two friends. They reveal Henry instantly as a soul mate, someone whose sport with Becket has its own marvelous freedoms.

The intimacy of the two male friends is something the monk-king, Louis, tries in vain to fathom. But there is also a wariness in friendship's celebrant, something almost furtive, that makes Henry's glimpse into his past only a glimpse, a truth he is half resolved to hide. We are surprised he should say as much as he does, and so is Henry, especially since his auditor, Louis, is "too cold to know the fashion" of love's freedoms. When Henry discloses his former hope that he and Becket could have been "Two sisters gliding in an equal dance, / Two rivers gently flowing side by side" (I. iii, Vol. 9, p. 60), it is hard not to find in this astonishing parenthesis a drama of repressed affection and sexual reversal, held in an excitable state of tension. In the "Prologue" Becket had claimed that Henry befriended him, "not as a statesman," but as a "true lover." Here, as in a choral soliloquy, Henry reveals a whole new dimension to the action: the capacity of two men to hate and love each other simultaneously. Tennyson's impartiality allows him to speak passionately on behalf of both men.

One reason why Tennyson excels in writing monologues should now be clear. A self-divided mind like Henry's is more capable of being explored in a monologue like "Tithonus" or "Ulysses" than in a stage play like *Becket.* No historical drama can be composed entirely of moments of psychological breakthrough in which the playwright conscripts a character to convey information that is not fully accessible to the character himself. But this kind of self-characterizing speech, in which a speaker like Henry is only subliminally aware of what he is characterizing, is a defining feature of dramatic monologues, where disclosures are often inadvertent or involuntary. Because St. Simeon Stylites' most important revelations are unconscious, we can hear him telling one story about himself while Tennyson is telling an ironically different story.

We are closest to Tennyson's speakers when they relax their will and momentarily allow the free vagrancy of their consciousness to suspend their role-playing. As in a lyrical monologue, Becket sometimes finds himself momentarily outside the dramatic action, in a different world—the world that might have been.

> Better have been
> A fisherman at Bosham, my good Herbert,
> Thy birthplace—the sea-creek—the petty rill
> That falls into it—the green field—the gray church—
> The simple lobster-basket, and the mesh—
> The more or less of daily labour done—
> The pretty gaping bills in the home-nest
> Piping for bread—the daily want supplied—
> The daily pleasure to supply it.
>
> (II. ii. Vol. 9, p. 111)

As the imagination wanders, so does the syntax. Its loose inventory of workaday maritime impressions seems as innocent of contrivance as the early-age wonder of marvels and commonplaces it freshly evokes. However unexpected, there is a pause here, as Becket and the audience stop to enjoy a moment of effortless pleasure. Such idyllic asides are like intermissions in a play: the role-player who acts out his fantasies of martyrdom momentarily imagines an alternative play in which he might perform a different role. Or he may briefly contemplate the pleasures of renouncing play-acting altogether.

As the climax of his tragedy approaches, Becket has nothing better to do than discuss the discovery of a fowl's nest or the death from leprosy of a fair-haired Norman maid, the world's lily, who once lived in his mother's house (V. ii).

> I once was out with Henry in the days
> When Henry loved me, and we came upon
> A wild-fowl sitting on her nest, so still
> I reached my hand and touched; she did not stir;
> The snow had frozen round her, and she sat
> Stone-dead upon a heap of ice-cold eggs.
> Look! how this love, this mother, runs through all
> The world God made—even the beast—the bird!
>   (V. ii, vol. 9, p. 185)

These digressions, with their flickers of gratuitous beauty and pathos, are the recollections of someone who seems to have forgotten what the play is about. The disturbing imperatives of impending martyrdom are never totally ignored, but they are also subtly resisted, as if there were something ill about the martyr's heart. The stone-dead bird, frozen upon her heap of ice-cold eggs, like the death by leprosy of the little lily, are oddly consoling to the martyr whose own role seems thrust upon him from outside, as one of the necessities of a tragic outcome.

We are most intimate with Tennyson's speakers when the reflexive understanding they display is too subtle or multilevelled for a stage play to dramatize. Nothing in *Becket* and *Queen Mary,* for example, is quite so touching or dramatic as the unactable moment in his idyll, "Lancelot and Elaine," when Lancelot knows that Elaine is looking at him, and Elaine is conscious that he knows.

> Then, when she heard his horse upon the stones,
> Unclasping flung the casement back, and looked
> Down on his helm, from which her sleeve had gone.
> And Lancelot knew the little clinking sound;
> And she by tact of love was well aware
> That Lancelot knew that she was looking at him.
>   ("Lancelot and Elaine," ll.973–78)

A stage play offers little opportunity for one-sided looking. Like the silent auditor in a monologue, however, Lancelot is not allowed to see or speak. When Elaine looks at him, she reduces him to the quintessential object. Ashamed to return her look, he cannot disarm her unstated censure by making her an object of his own gaze. The best comment on the passage comes from Christopher Ricks: "The tact, the tenderness, the unmentioned bruises: to me the lines are unforgettable."[3] As in Tennyson's monologue "Tithonus," however, where the speaker looks forward to a time when he can withhold his look from the goddess who must still look down on his grave—

> Thou seëst all things, thou wilt see my grave;
> Thou wilt renew thy beauty morn by morn,
> I earth in earth forget these empty courts,
> And thee returning on thy silver wheels
>   ("Tithonus," ll.73–76)

the true poignancies of this drama are too multiple and reflexive to be transferred to the stage.

When a speaker like the lover in *Maud*, instead of acting a single dramatic part, acts out a series of fantasies, the very freedoms of invention that unsuit him for the role of avenging his father's suicide may make us as unexpectedly intimate with him as we are with Shakespeare's Hamlet. Though Maud's lover sounds at times like a Byronic stereotype, his splendid tirades in the Byronic manner are only one of many roles he improvises. At first the heavy halting spondees match the heavy heart of a misanthrope and outcast. But with a slight alteration in the stresses the speaker can intimate the smooth beginnings of release, rising with a half-stormy sweep to his apparition of Maud's "Passionless, pale, cold face, star-sweet on a gloom profound" (I. 91). As despair returns, the speaker seeks refuge in agnostic theology, whose drift is as veiled as his own love for Maud. After experimenting with the serenity of a woodland philosopher, far removed from the "clamour of liars," the heavy beats slide back again, culminating in a fling of resolute defiance, lightened by an alliterating lift in the stanza's final line: "You have but fed on the roses and lain in the lilies of life" (I. 161).

Such a myriad-minded speaker's roles and interests are as diverse as his meters, some exploiting the deliberate dullness of near-doggerel and some as wild in their rhythmical freedom as the lover's widely ranging passions and quick fluctuations of mood. As a result of such diversity, he is a more vivid but also more ambiguous figure than the Byronic lover in "Locksley Hall." When he thinks of Maud's father coming to the two corpses in the pit—the corpses of Maud and her brother, he says that he "could even weep to think of it" (II.324). At this moment the lover is confusing Maud's father with his own father, a suicide victim for whom Maud's father once "laid a cruel snare in a pit" (II.322). Unpredictable in his confusion of friend and enemy, and touching in his power to weep for old foes, Maud's lover shows how different moments in his past may flash out unexpectedly, making him far more complex than a standard Byronic hero.

We become intimate with Maud's lover partly because of the flashover effects that confuse the wheels that go over his head in the madhouse with the motion of "the dancers dancing in tune" to the music in the garden just before the duel (I.865). Other brief flashovers, such as the metrical identity of the horses' pounding hooves—"And the hoofs of the horses beat, beat" (II.246)—with the pounding of the lover's own heart as he waits for Maud in the garden—"She is near, she is near," "I hear, I hear" (I.912, 914)—preserve those vagaries of the inner life which make us share a speaker's consciousness and which are precluded by the case history of a fanatic like St. Simeon or a Byronic stereotype like the lover in "Locksley Hall."

Even the lotos-eaters exhibit in their choral song a shocking discrepancy between the lure of family life in Ithaca and the attractions of lotos-land. In the long epic simile of their final chorus, the lotos-eaters can never quite get over their amazed surprise at choosing the indolence of epicurean deities over the challenges of "an ill-used race of men that cleave the soil" ("The Lotos-Eaters," l.165). The free vagrancy of their memories, which dwell fondly on their "wedded lives" and "the last embraces of [their] wives" (ll.114–15), continue to absorb them in the most rewarding of human pleasures. How, then, can they imprison their wandering consciousness by imitating the self-absorption of cruel and indifferent deities? The mariners' deep and backward-reaching intimacies ill equip them for the monotonies of lotos-land, to which their decision never to "wander more" (l.173) commits them. Though their flesh and spirit crave a relaxation of their wills, they also realize that a soft paradise would be vastly inferior to the strenuous life at sea that has always galvanized them.

In his greatest monologues Tennyson finds a tragic reality as far away as possible from such distressing events as Hallam's death or the suicidal melancholia of his own father, and yet intimately in contact with them. Though Tennyson writes as the most personal of poets in *In Memoriam* and a few of his elegies, normally he can treat grief, despair, and elation most successfully, not in his lyrics, but in the more distant and formal medium of his mythical and historical monologues.

The poet-ventriloquist behind the masks of these monologues can be most himself when he is someone else. These poems never begin at home, which is where the "sincere" confessional poet feels he must begin. Instead, the poet-ventriloquist of the monologues and monodramas is as free as Shakespeare's Ariel to exercise his magic by remote control. In *Maud* the exiled speaker's freedom to count the whorls of the shell as a stay against confusion makes us specially conscious of this power. It is the same kind of awareness that beguiles Ulysses as he imagines himself passing freely beyond the utmost bound of human thought. To be conscious of this freedom, and yet to feel anxious about the adventurous imaginative life one must lead in order to possess it, is the source of Tennyson's double irony, which discloses the contending possibilities among which self-divided characters like Ulysses, Maud's lover, and even the lotos-eaters have to live.

Often the unvoiced apprehensions in these monologues are more important than anything a speaker says. Though Tennyson's understanding of Tithonus' incongruous demands is unexpressed, it can be inferred from Aurora's silent smile when he asks for immortality. Even Ulysses is oddly ambivalent in his muted tribute to Telemachus: "He works his work, I mine" (l.43). Heroic leave-taking is eminently actable. But the unsuitability for acting of the family situation and the family emotions (what must Telemachus and the long suffering Penelope be thinking of Ulysses?) is apparent not only in the son's silence but also in the father's studied ambiguity about how he is to speak to (and of) his son.

Because King Arthur, like many virtuous people, is not interesting to hear, see, or talk to, and is tedious in himself, he cannot be taken over by an actor. And yet his vacancy as a character is the deepest and most affecting truth about his domestic life. Surrounded by evil and the excitements of intrigue, which throw into dramatic relief his own inability to play a role, Arthur shows us something more important than inveterate actors or off-stage performers like Guinevere and Lancelot, who are perfectly at home in the world of playacting. Arthur reminds us of the unrelenting bathos and horror of a family situation which cannot bear talking about, much less acting up to or acting out. Indeed, if Arthur were a better actor, his tragedy would be less authentic and also less moving than it is.

For Ulysses and Lucretius, by contrast, being histrionic is as involuntary as breathing. The first words of their monologues immediately kindle dramatic interest. They make a deep dynamic impression. We are eager to follow their activity, because we hope, as one critic says, that "our rapt curiosity [will soon be] replaced by the satisfaction of insight."[4]

> It little profits that an idle king,
> By this still hearth, among these barren crags,
> Matched with an agèd wife, I mete and dole
> Unequal laws unto a savage race,
> That hoard, and sleep, and feed, and know not me.
>   ("Ulysses," ll.1–5)

> Storm in the night! for thrice I heard the rain
> Rushing; and once the flash of a thunderbolt—
> Methought I never saw so fierce a fork—
>   ("Lucretius," ll.26–28)

Readers are beguiled in Ulysses' opening lines by a commanding voice that concedes its own incapacity for command. Having echoed the indecisive Hamlet in line five (*Hamlet* iv.35), what self-contradiction or paradox, we wonder, will this oddly ineffectual ruler utter next? A few moments later his highly allusive reflection: "How dull it is to pause, to make an end, / To rust unburnished, not to shine in use!" (ll.22–23) lends authority to his words even as it conspires to challenge that authority by dramatizing another two-way pull between adventure and repose, heroic resolve and a suicidal voyage into death.

These incongruous effects are achieved, partly because Ulysses echoes the irresolute Hamlet again (IV.iv.39), but also because his words resonate with Othello's command to Brabantio, which it manages—unobtrusively but brilliantly—to reverse: "Keep up your bright swords, for the dew will rust them" (*Othello* I.ii.59). We hear Ulysses hovering between a stable moral self and a histrionic self that dangerously detonates, splitting into fragments. At the moment such a speaker seems about to attain his goal, he begins to fade into his own audience, becoming a spectator of his descent into the underworld or of his death at sea, just as the king in "The Passing of Arthur" is replaced at the climax of his monologue by a bewildered Bedivere, and just as Galahad in "The

Holy Grail" is seen through the eyes of a puzzled, only half-comprehending Percivale.

The suspense that attends Lucretius' opening words is deepened when he discloses an instant later that the real geography of the violent setting he evokes is a geography of his mind: "Storm, and what dreams, ye holy Gods, what dreams! / For thrice I wakened after dreams" (ll.33–34). The "flaming atom-streams" of a universe in dissolution, "Ruining along the illimitable inane" (ll.38, 40), describe with fine precision the agitated mental state of a Roman Heathcliff, someone who immediately interests us because of his strong but disintegrating personality. Often we feel that the drama of such a self-divided consciousness is exploding on the stage of Tennyson's own mind and is about to spill over into the private theater of *our* minds, too.

Our intimacy with speakers like Ulysses and Lucretius, who easily engage our imaginations, is not to be confused with our detachment from such case studies in abnormal psychology as St. Simeon Stylites, the Byronic hero of "Locksley Hall," or the daughters of Hesperus. There is a difference between Simeon's inability to be a convincing martyr and Lucretius' failure to establish a philosophic system that will satisfy his imagination without insulting his intelligence. In Lucretius' case, as in the aged Ulysses' desire to be a youthful adventurer and the desire of Tithonus, the lover of the beautiful, to be immortal, the double ironies and surprises turn out to be invigorating and engaging in themselves. By contrast, there is little compelling about the comic obsessions of St. Simeon, the dethroned saint and humanized charlatan, or about the disillusionments of the self-absorbed lover in "Locksley Hall," who is too obviously an impersonal Byronic stereotype to involve us.

The more intimate we become with speakers unsuited for their roles, the more vulnerable they seem. The lover's vulnerability in *Maud* is partly a result of there being no background and no middle distance in his mind. A ghostly apparition in the sky and a tiny "miracle of design" like the shell come forward with equally aggressive clearness. Even when the lover goes into exile, however, the freedom of consciousness that allows him to combine the delicacy of a dream with a scientist's sharp accuracy in tracing out the whorls of the shell reveals something very important about his mind.

> Slight, to be crushed with a tap
> Of my finger-nail on the sand
> (*Maud* II.69–70)

> Strange, that the mind, when fraught
> With a passion so intense
>   (*Maud* II.106–7)

Evoked in the same metrical form as the shell, the speaker's mind proves to be an equally fragile but resilient "miracle of design."

Tennyson's Ulysses is a more complicated case. In a moment of melancholy reflection that relaxes his will, Ulysses tries to convince himself how ill-suited he is to ease into death, even in old age. The poem originates in a peaceful twilight mood that it then tries vigorously to repudiate. For the epic convention of the blunt, plain-spoken mariner, Ulysses the orator substitutes his own rhetorical conventions of false reticence and denial. A self-deprecating modesty can be heard in his double negative, "Not unbecoming," and in his negative definition: "Myself not least" (ll.53, 15). Even his most ringing and sonorous phrases are studiously indirect: "know not me," "not to fail," "not to yield" (ll.5, 40, 70).

Ulysses' truths are most compromising and equivocal when they seem to be frankest and most open. For example, his exhortations, "Come, my friends," "Push off" (ll.56, 58), appear to discard artifice for a candor and directness that any comrade might respond to. But the voyage into "gulfs" that "will wash" the mariners "down" (l.62), or into the Homeric underworld where they may see the great Achilles, is also a suicide mission that signals the end rather than the beginning of experience. As Ulysses fades with the ever-shifting margin or sinks with the star "Beyond the utmost bound of human thought" (l.32), the vocatives restore (rather than simply repudiate or efface) the precise and grave mystery of oblivion in everything. Because of the poised repose that suspends Ulysses between resolve and resignation, his concluding switch from artifice to directness may be less direct—less frank and open—than it seems.

Though Simeon is ill equipped for his dramatic part, his case study in martyrdom (however farcical or grotesque it may be) makes him less vulnerable than characters like Lucretius or the lotos-eaters, who remain unconscious of just how unsuited to their roles they really are. Ulysses' unconsciousness of being too old for another voyage is precisely what brings us into his mind, making it as far as possible our own. Few old people truly grasp that they are old, and in being cast as an ancient ruler, matched with an "agèd wife," Ulysses is asked to play a role that he, like most old people, never fully believes in.

By contrast, Simeon, like Amy's lover in "Locksley Hall," can adjust his role-playing to the action's demands with wonderful agility. If a miracle is an event which creates faith, as Simeon shrewdly intimates, then even in looking on a spiritual con man like himself, the faithful may learn to look through a fraudulent mask and see God behind it. Some real experience of God may lie at the heart of Simeon's deception. Tennyson is not just dethroning a saint in order to humanize a scoundrel. Even after he has lost his dignity and honor, Simeon offers a testimony to his religion that no mere impostor could offer:

> for you may look on me,
> And in your looking you may kneel to God.
> ("St. Simeon Stylites," ll.138–39)

Like Chaucer's Pardoner, Simeon is marvelously adept at the role he plays. Because he knows he is fanatical enough to be a martyr but not spiritual enough to be a saint, Simeon can deflect the criticisms he anticipates. In most of the other monologues the portrayal of a consciousness that is unsuited to its destiny is much subtler because less self-aware than Simeon's. Whereas Simeon is a deceiver who is also more than a deceiver, Tithonus in his quest for immortality and Ulysses in his heroic evasion of death are unwitting *self*-deceivers. Their moments of deception are also our moments of greatest intimacy with them.

Chapter Seven

Acting Versus Acting Out: Fantasy and the Monologues

Richard Wollheim makes an important distinction between "acting" a dramatic part that can be challenged or tested and "acting out" a fantasy.[1] To "act" the role of a martyr in a stage play like *Becket* is to be challenged and "heckled." It is to be asked if the desire to become a martyr is not incompatible with the attainment of that state. The satisfactions of a play are never wholly internal: performances can never be totally rehearsed or invulnerable to another actor's challenge. By contrast, to "act out" a fantasy of martyrdom in a dramatic monologue like "St. Simeon Stylites" is to substitute for an open-ended action the closed enactment of an *idée fixe* or obsession. It is to forfeit the chance of being proved righteous by avoiding the risk of being proved a sham.

"Acting out" a fantasy is to a speaker's performance in a dramatic monologue what the "acting" of a dramatic part is to a character's performance in a stage play. Preserved from testing, and entirely inward, the fantasies of an aspiring martyr like Becket or of a fanatic like Queen Mary seem to have wandered into the stage plays from a different genre. Such obsessions are more congenial to a monologue or monodrama, where the defects of playacting, fantasy-creation, and the loss of self-identity through verbal trickery can be more readily dramatized and exposed for what they are.

A character in a play should be responsive to people whose resistance to his fantasies might set up a counter-action. But as early as the first scene, Tennyson's Becket says he is "martyr in [himself] already." Though Becket's most important motives are the most elusive and obscure, in seeking martyrdom he seems to be inventing a role for himself that can pit him against Henry, his unfaithful soul mate and brother. He is more resolved to cross Henry's will than make love to Henry's substitute, "Our holy mother Canterbury," a woman "who sits / With tattered robes," destitute and despised (I.i, vol. 9, p. 29).

When Walter Map attacks Becket for acting out a melodrama of rehearsed opposition to the king's conciliatory overtures, Becket cries out:

The State will die, the Church can never die . . .
But I must die for that which never dies.
I will be so — my visions in the Lord:
. . . And there, there, there, not here I shall rejoice
To find my stray sheep back within the fold.

(III.iii, vol. 9, p. 146)

In a sense, Becket is more in love with the idea of dying than with the cause for which he dies. He is resolved to sacrifice political complexities to the clinching force of an antithesis. His agitation and confusion are nowhere more evident than in his frantic use of ostensive definition: "And there, there, there, not here I shall rejoice." Closer to the hysteria of Browning's delinquent Caliban, cowering in fear as he counts off another lightning bolt, than to the confident faith of Milton's swain, glorying in the promise of paradise at the climax of "Lycidas," Becket's fantasies of martyrdom seem anxious to conceal an obscure illness: an unnamed mental or spiritual affliction.

Acting out a fantasy of martyrdom, a monologue like "St. Simeon Stylites" is unimpeded by any counteraction: it lacks the antiphonal voice of a "heckler." Though such voices can be heard in Tennyson's play *Queen Mary,* they have no effect on Mary's resolve to wed Philip and secure the succession of a Catholic heir. The honest and dishonest responses to the portrait of Philip that Mary shows Gardiner, the French ambassador, and later Simon Renard, set up their own compliance in and resistance to Mary's unshakable fantasy of falling in love, not with a flesh-and-blood prince, but with an icon. Like the picture of George Osborne which becomes part of Amelia's portable household shrine in *Vanity Fair,* Philip's portrait is one of Mary's palace idols. It is also a metaphor for the distorting fantasy she is determined to act out in defiance of all counsel to the contrary.

Fantasies that may be challenged in a stage play can be indulged with greater impunity in a dramatic monologue or monodrama. Acting out a fantasy of martyrdom allows Tennyson's St. Simeon Stylites to remake his life. The event-fantasy of the saint's dying gloriously—or ingloriously—on his pillar is imposed on the world as a scenario the speaker would like to rehearse or "act out" in Wollheim's sense. In the absence of any explicit criticism of the speaker, readers themselves are left to test his fantasy. They are meant to see how Simeon debases the scriptural prophecy that the last shall be first by acting out, at the very summit of a pillar, his fiction of being lowly and least. Taking the biblical text too literally, he falsifies its truth. Simeon's contempt for the body is also a form of worshipping the body. By enslaving himself to his ulcerous sores and loathsome physical decay, he cultivates a perverse inversion of the pleasure principle he claims to scorn. Everything he does and says thinly masks contradictions of humility and arrogance, asceticism and sensuality, of satisfactions achieved in an intensely private theater of his mind and satisfactions flaunted publicly on a stage.

By acting out a fantasy the speaker preserves it, and in preserving the fantasy he preserves the contradictory desires it contains. St. Simeon acts out his fantasy of expiring slowly on his pillar because it preserves his desire both to loathe and take pleasure in the pains of the flesh. Maud's lover acts out his fantasy of avenging his father's suicide because it preserves his desire both to hate and love her cold and luminous beauty. As a Victorian Hamlet, the lover can conceal the competing desires of his fantasy by playing the role of his father's avenger: he loves the girl but hates her family. In killing Maud's brother and causing Maud's own death, the lover can misrepresent his masochistic desire to destroy and hate what he loves as a natural correction of his earlier idolatry of Maud, whom he celebrates in the sacramental language of the Song of Songs and in some of the most ostentatious love poetry in the English language.

To conceal the fact that his simultaneous hate and love are competing desires, the angry young man in "Locksley Hall" splits up his fantasies into two distinct narratives. The fantasy of becoming a South-Sea savage, a sort of Tarzan, distills a desire to protect Amy. But the protector's denunciation of the shallow woman he once professed to love, like Heathcliff's denunciation of Cathy and Linton in *Wuthering Heights,* also allows us to see the two sides of his relation to Amy in a single obsessional act.

If Simeon did not routinely ascend his pillar day after day, and if the lover in *Maud* did not maintain a protective fiction of hating Maud long after he had fallen in love with her, these speakers might begin to test their fantasies. To become their internal observers is to adopt the view of critical readers, who may find what they see bizarre, grotesque, deranged, or untrue.

But as Wollheim explains, every time a fantasy is acted out it will seem more normal to the speaker. This is why the lover's belief that he hates what he loves and loves what he hates becomes a little more secure against the threat of criticism each time he rails against Maud's brother or father, or each time the ghastly glimmer of Maud's ghost appears to him like lightning under the stars.

Acting out dual roles also strengthens the disguise with which the angry young man in "Locksley Hall" conceals his desire to be rid of Amy and the burden of domestic responsibilities assumed by his successful rival. The fantasy allows the speaker to luxuriate in his despair and justify his escapist impulses. Similarly, in *Maud*, acting out the roles of Romeo and Hamlet, the lover can disguise his desire to exorcise Maud's demon and be rid forever of the curse of Maud's family, which has tormented both himself and his father. By concealing desires both fantasies abet self-ignorance. They may even lead to self-error by encouraging both speakers to lay claim to amorous desires they do not have. Maud is worshipped as the second Eve, the virgin of the *hortus conclusus* in the Song of Songs, rather than as a flesh-and-blood woman; and before being coldly anatomized for her small but selfish faults, Amy is first extolled as a soul mate and altruist whose service is perfect freedom.

The fantasies also provide substitute satisfactions for the escapist desires they contain. Killing Maud's brother in a duel and causing Maud's death are the lover's thwarted attempts to escape from Maud and to banish her family from his memory. And imagining Amy to regret her choice of a shallow husband is the speaker's thwarted attempt to transfer to her his own secret desire to escape the trap of marriage, which his fiction of being the rejected, long-suffering suitor prevents his openly admitting.

Though an interior monologue like *Maud* is well suited to the acting out of fantasies, it may also contain an authentic action inside the role-playing. The angry young man in "Locksley Hall" may be in love with the idea of loving Amy. But like Romeo's infatuation with Rosaline, his idolatry of Amy is incapable of progressing from make-believe to action. Preferring to be free, he may even seem grateful that he is not taken at his word and that his professions of love are not reciprocated. In *Maud*, by contrast, the speaker vigorously pursues the woman. Like Romeo's active courtship of Juliet, which contrasts with his retreat into a forest when fantasizing about his undeclared love for Rosaline, the lover in *Maud* exhorts his beloved to come into the garden and later consummate their love. As Wollheim explains, "the desires that a fantasy contains are never tested in the acting out of the fantasy. . . . No joy can be expected" from the speaker's denunciation of Amy; the most he can hope for is "relief."[2]

Poised, by contrast, between hope and fear, and tense with expectation, the lover in *Maud* puts his imagination of love to the test. Acting

out his fantasy of being avenged on Maud's family is unlikely to bring
him any deep pleasure. But in acting rather than acting out, the lover is
no longer projecting a fantasy upon the world but seeing how the world
itself will respond. The intense pleasure the lover anticipates depends
on his going outside himself. In Wollheim's words, "in acting out, pleasure has been fully anticipated and fully discounted." The speaker's
desire to be avenged on Amy or Maud "is not exposed to the fresh air of
experience." In the case of a dramatic action, however, including the
lover's impassioned courtship of Maud, "the way in which a desire is
tested, or confirmed or rejected as corresponding to what the person
really wants, is in large part a matter of the pleasure that its satisfaction
brings with it."[3]

When Simeon acts out his fantasy of being ascetic, he remains self-
ignorant of the hedonism that allows him to derive a perverse physical
pleasure from his pain. In his self-ignorance he is not aware of his desire
to be glorified by being humiliated, or of striving to be exalted by pretending to be low and abased. In his self-error he also attributes to himself a desire to be a theological model, a pattern or example to the religious community.

> But thou, O Lord,
> Aid all this foolish people; let them take
> Example, pattern: lead them to thy light.
> ("St. Simeon Stylites," ll.218–20)

As a self-centered masochist, Simeon cannot experience the pure selfless-
ness of a true martyr. But stories of martyrdom allow him to conceal his
real motives. And because they are rich in fantasy, they appeal to both
Simeon's and Tennyson's theatrical sense. Richard Wollheim goes further
by ingeniously attributing the "self-error" of such an actor to his "loan"
from the martyr's rich repertoire of dramatic parts.[4]

Wollheim's distinction between "self-ignorance" and "self-error" also
applies to the angry young rebel in "Locksley Hall." In acting out his
fantasy of being a jilted lover whose loss is unparalleled, he remains "self-
ignorant" of his desire to escape social responsibility by renouncing Amy.
Though he would rather be a self-exiled Bohemian than a reliable
defender of the status quo, he has to conceal that preference, even from
himself. Borrowing the rhetoric of a Byronic hero, he uses political radicalism and moral outrage to perpetuate the error he himself has

authored. The blustering youth is not really a Byronic Cain or Satan at war with God and the universe. But it is consoling to take refuge in such heroic fictions, especially since their rhetoric is a mask behind whose bravura the rebel's smug assumptions of superior integrity can be partly hidden.

When the old Northern farmer acts out his fantasy of being a corner-stone of the rural hierarchy, he remains "self-ignorant" of the irony that he is trying to dislodge a more important cornerstone. The farmer incon-gruously mixes two biblical roles: the role of the faithful laborer in the vineyard and the role of the querulous psalmist, questioning God's ways to man. Because his services are indispensable to the local squire, he can-not see why the squire of the universe should consent to remove him. He secretly blames God for failing to reverse the doom of man for him alone. In trying to decide what he really feels about becoming part of "the unhonored dead," the old farmer borrows the story line of the polit-ical conservative. But since death the leveler is a political radical, the old man contrives to conceal the politics of death behind the rich and actable fantasies of laissez-faire doctrine, a conservative ideology that opposes most forms of revolution, including the ultimate leveling of death itself.

In acting out his fantasies of ownership, the new Northern farmer also remains self-ignorant of his desire to exercise power by acquiring wealth. In his self-ignorance Tennyson's speaker fails to register the irony that the provident father is also a proprietary tyrant. To conceal his pride of ownership, the farmer adopts the conventional role of a capitalist, eager to annex adjacent lands by marrying his son to a local heiress. That role guarantees self-error, however, for it conceals behind a desire to own property a desire to set up a tyranny within his own domestic circle.

Chapter Eight

The Uses of Casuistry: Bad Faith and Irony

Though "acting out a fantasy" is a distinguishing feature of several of Tennyson's best dramatic monologues and of his monodrama, *Maud*, Tennyson knows that even when casuists like the lover in "Locksley Hall" set out to tell lies, they cannot helping telling some portion of the truth as well. To know what excuses might justify Ulysses in abandoning his family or what arguments Lucretius might use to rationalize his suicide is not to be callously indifferent to virtue. Only a keen admirer of truth is capable of seeking and finding it like Tennyson in the obscurest regions of special pleading and bad faith.

St. Simeon's bad faith takes the form of lying to himself. Though his lofty pillar discredits his fantasy of being low and abased, his deception is not to be confused with lying in general. He is not a master of deception like Chaucer's Pardoner, who tries to sell worthless relics to the pilgrims. Because the Pardoner's lies mask the truth, he has first to possess the truth he is hiding. By contrast, Simeon's bad faith hides the truth from himself. The deception of the proud hedonist masquerading as an abased saint is an irony of which Simeon himself is only subliminally aware.

Paris's infidelity to Tennyson's Oenone or Guinevere's to Arthur posits a duality of deceiver and deceived. But bad faith implies the unity of a single consciousness. Aurora lies to Tithonus about the nature of the immortality she agrees to confer on him. Like the speakers in "Locksley Hall" and *Maud*, however, Tennyson's Lucretius and his lotos-eaters lie only to themselves. In "bad faith," as Sartre defines the term,[1] the deceiver and the dupe are one and the same person. The lotos-eaters try to trick themselves into believing that life in lotos-land is worthy of them. Tennyson's Lucretius, face to face with nothingness, possesses in his capacity as a poet and cosmologist the truths which are hidden from him in his official capacity as a materialist philosopher and atheist. For Tennyson, the poet behind the mask, Lucretius the disenchanted unbeliever—the unraveler of other people's deceptions—is himself self-deceived. As John Keble explains in his *Oxford Lectures on Poetry,* which Tennyson owned, Lucretius was a believer without knowing he believed.[2]

If the lover in *Maud* is to conceal from himself the truth that he is already in love with Maud, he must know this truth very exactly himself in order to maintain the protective fiction that he hates her. The anguish of Tennyson's dying Lucretius seems genuine. But the despair of the jilted lovers in *Maud* and "Locksley Hall," like the anguish of St. Simeon, decaying by slow degrees on his pillar, is a mere mask of anguish. Such speakers "act out" a fantasy of anguish in order to escape genuine despair.

Despite the energy with which the angry young men in "Locksley Hall" and *Maud* play their roles of outcast and victim, the near hysteria of their rhetoric keeps betraying them, even to themselves. They both know and don't know they are liars. Dickens' Pip observes that the greatest of swindlers is the self-swindler. Certainly, self-deceivers like the Byronic heroes in "Locksley Hall" and *Maud*, or like the lotos-eaters, are more dangerous than simple liars like Chaucer's Pardoner or Browning's Mr. Sludge, the medium. The essence of bad faith is that the person who lies to himself is honest and sincere. Such a speaker's project would fail completely if he were deliberately and cynically to lie to himself.

In the sequel to "Locksley Hall," "Locksley Hall Sixty Years After," the speaker acknowledges the irony, already implicit in the earlier monologue, that the ranter was a lesser person than his rival and that his egotism blinded him to the fact that he was too immature to marry. Though the eighty-year-old speaker is sorry he rejected his dead rival's conciliatory gesture (1.256), acknowledging that he should have acted with more grace and self-command, he is still the same old egoist, quick to reject the comparison of his grandson's "boy-love" to his own (1.6). Masking his self-conceit behind protests that "the modern amourist is of easier, earlier make" (1.18), the grandfather still censors truths that might embarrass or disturb the rousing Byronic performance he feels called upon to give. Even in conceding that he himself has "often babbled . . . of a foolish past" (1.7), the grandfather is also conscious of repressing unflattering qualities in himself in order not to be conscious of them. Such unconscious self-deception is exactly what Sartre means by bad faith.[3]

The rebel in "Locksley Hall" may be admired as a paradigm of lofty ideals and disillusionment, of splendid purposes doomed to failure in an imperfect world. But though his speech may be impressive, it can hardly be moving, for it is largely impersonal. The people to be pitied in "Locksley Hall Sixty Years After" are not the speaker but the berated

Amy, who dies in childbirth, and her ill-fated husband, who never remarries. Readers tend to lose interest in the speaker's large Byronic postures and expansive gestures. Compared with the invigorating surprises in *Maud*, where the demented lover confuses Maud's dead father with his own father toward the end of the monodrama and where revenge gives way to compassion and even love, the speaker in "Locksley Hall" is a hollow stereotype. There is nothing for him to do but go through the motions of Byronic piety. His tirades depend on a predictable decorum, and though he thinks his decison to emigrate has a noble logic to it, the flatness and one-dimensional finality of his attitudes are a dramatic disaster.

The grating deliberation of his long rolling hexameters reveals little about the Byronic speaker, beyond the fact that he feels wounded and enraged and that he exacerbates his wound by dwelling on the lusts of his actively amorous rival.

> As the husband is, the wife is: thou art mated with a clown,
> And the grossness of his nature will have weight to drag thee down.
> ("Locksley Hall," ll.47–48)

His raging is the standard sort of Byronic tirade, full of gusto and virtuosity but deficient in any nuances or subtleties of tone. Byronic idealism and the splendid disillusionment that goes with it would be excellent things, Tennyson seems to be saying, if only human beings were capable of them. This perhaps is why the shrill assertiveness of Amy's lover is never quite convincing and never rings true.

The contrast with Maud's lover is instructive. When the speaker in *Maud* launches into his Byronic tirades, we see into aspects of his life— his filial love, his self-divided mind, his incapacity for revenge—that are all the more intimate and absorbing because of the story line's apparent indifference to them. Tennyson understands the adolescent bravura of both lovers. But in exploring the nature and motives of Maud's lover, he finds ways of making us feel what the desire to be avenged involves. He then shows why the lover, like Hamlet, has far too much negative capability to be an effective avenger. Tennyson expands this tragic unsuitability into the plot of the double suicide, the death of Maud's brother in the duel, and the treatment of a dramatically motivated (as opposed to a merely self-imposed) exile.

Whereas the torment of Maud's lover touches us directly, as he tries to ward off confusion by counting the whorls of the shell as an exile in

Brittany or as he attains a precariously lucid but hard-won state of grace after his mental breakdown, the suffering of Amy's lover touches us only obliquely or hardly at all. The speaker is hurt, and that can be moving. But there is something indulgent about his hurt and his longing to be loved. His nostalgia for Utopia is the yearning of a child for the haven of an unreal paradise—a golden age. Yet out of this childlike and confused apprehension nothing comparable to the transformation of Maud's lover emerges. His flat tirades and empty rhetoric prevent it.

In "Locksley Hall" the falling trochees and ranting couplets of the long, rolling fifteeners create a histrionic effect that shows up the falsity and sensationalism of the stories the lover keeps telling himself. There are occasional felicities, however, especially when the gridlock of the end-stopped couplets is broken, and a rare run-on line combines with a relaxed hyperbaton and a triad of hyphenated compounds to dramatize a momentary release into the pleasures of what Arthur O. Lovejoy calls "soft pastoralism."

> Droops the heavy-blossomed bower, hangs the heavy-fruited-tree—
> Summer isles of Eden lying in dark-purple spheres of sea.
> ("Locksley Hall," ll.163–64)

Just as the cumbersome couplets turn on the hinges of heavy caesural pauses, so the soldier-lover swings ponderously from Romantic optimism to Malthusian pessimism. He fluctuates between the nostalgias of dream—of lost love, innocence, and paradise—and obsessed repetitions of disillusion and cynicism.

The lover's denunciation of Amy and his half-comic ranting are occasionally brought short by his own amused self-criticism: "Well—'tis well that I should bluster!" (l.63). But generally he is taken in by his own lies. He is the duped victim as well as the deceiver, powerless to suspend his predictable fluctuations between Utopian dream and harsh awakening, between wishing or praying for a better world and a chastened acceptance of the world as it is.

Though he is a virulent antifeminist, denouncing "Woman" as "the lesser man" (l.151), the lover also wants to play Heathcliff to Amy's Catherine. Like Brontë's lovers, the two cousins were soul mates as children, siblings rather than strangers. Moreover, as the ward of a selfish uncle after his father's death in India, the lover, like Heathcliff, is an orphan raised by an uncongenial father substitute. Written in 1837–1838, the monologue may influence *Wuthering Heights* (1847), whose Byronic hero denounces Linton in the same terms Tennyson's speaker denounces his rival. Amy's real betrayal is a self-betrayal: and the fate that awaits her, death in childbirth, though not disclosed until the sequel, makes the parallels between Cathy and Amy, Heathcliff and Tennyson's Byronic lover, all the more striking.

In "Northern Farmer, Old Style," Tennyson mutes the stridency of "Locksley Hall"'s trochees and dactyls by breaking up the long poetic lines into short syntactic units that coincide with the natural breaking points of the speaking voice. As the farmer issues brusque orders to his auditor: "Noorse? thourt nowt o'a noorse: whoy, Doctor's abeän an' agoän," (l.2), Tennyson throws all the stress of the opening dactyl onto the farmer's first-syllable vocative. The alliterative binding of the first three stresses, "noorse, nowt, noorse," also edges his address with good-humored contempt. When he displays raw humor in half boasting and half denying that he is the father of Bessy's child, the sharp caesural breaks allow the farmer to speak with a mixture of scorn and barely concealed pride:

> Bessy Marris's barne! tha knaws she laäid it to meä.
> Mowt a beän, mayhap, for she wur a bad un, sheä.
> ("Northern Farmer, Old Style," ll.21–22)

Trying to make a joke of his sexual trespass, he casts the woman in the role of his seducer. While admitting that he could never understand a sermon, he is genuinely intrigued by the parson's saying that "The amoighty's a taäkin o'you to 'issén, my friend" (l.26). Touched like a child by the mystery of his own mortality, the old man twice asks the nurse to explain it: why should God take *him*?

> Do godamoighty knaw what a's doing a-taäkin o' meä?
> I beänt wonn as saws 'ere a beän an' yonder a peä;
> An' Squoire 'ull be sa mad an' all—a' dear, a' dear!
> And I'a managed for Squoire coom Michaelmas thutty year.
> ("Northern Farmer, Old Style," ll.45–48)

The second line harbors an irony that passes over the old man's head. Since he has already boasted that Bessy's bairn may be his illegimate child, God may be taking the line more figuratively than the farmer intends. The double reference to the farmer's selfless loyalty to the squire also alerts the reader to a different use of "squire": in sowing a bean here and a pea there, the farmer has "squired" an heir. Inadvertently, this rustic Job seems to have answered his own question. As a private joke shared by Tennyson with his readers, the possibility that God is punishing the old farmer for sowing wild oats and then being in bad faith about his trespass lingers on as the poem's amusing afterthought.

The casuistry and bad faith that abound in Tennyson's monologues often allow the poet behind the masks to maintain an ironic distance from his speakers. Tithonus, for example, tries to model his passing into easeful death upon a Keatsian ideal of ceasing upon the midnight with no pain. But Tennyson expects us to know that Tithonus will not end his life with as much relaxed dignity as he ends his beautifully composed monologue: he will be turned ignominiously to an insect instead. Even in paying his last meticulous courtesies to the radiant Aurora, returning daily on her silver wheels, he is made the target of a second cruel joke.

When the speakers in "Locksley Hall" and *Maud* conclude with resounding dramatic effects, and even nature seems to cooperate with their pathetic fallacies by turning dark and menacing, we may feel that these contrived endings have still to be put to the test of how life is actually lived. A real-life drama tends to get its climaxes wrong, and often produces grotesque farces or comedies instead of the anticipated outcomes. The speaker's announcement of the proper end for himself in a melodrama of the sort he wants to act out is subtly but decisively challenged by the sequel to "Locksley Hall," which makes clear that the lover in the first poem is inferior to his rival and, despite his bitter complaints, altogether more prosperous and lucky.

Like Tithonus, Simeon tries to show that life has been a preparation for martyrdom: he is assured that everything will work out like an audit. Yet even in pronouncing that the end is at hand: "The end! the end! / Surely the end! (ll.198–99), the repetition of "end" refuses to end. And neither does St. Simeon's grotesque farce, which is protracted beyond the poem's anticipated limits. Tennyson parodies the last scene of *King Lear,* a play that refuses to end when it is expected to. Simeon's life, like Lear's, has been ready to end from the first verse paragraph, but it creeps on relentlessly in apparent defiance of the limits that are set for it.

We are made to feel that speakers like Tithonus and Simeon could bear a real martyrdom or a truly tragic death if it came to them with what Oscar Wilde calls "a purple pall and a mask of noble sorrow."[4] But the ending that life substitutes for their imagination of an ending seems prosaic and commonplace, with no redeeming dignity or trace of style. The aesthetic satisfaction of fitting our response to our fate is constantly thwarted, because life is a poor tragedian. At the climax of his real-life tragedy, when taken from court to prison, Wilde complains of the dramatic incongruities: it is a wet day, and he has few observers to applaud or appreciate the performance that he gives. Conversely, he has a full house when he least wants one. "Of all possible objects I was the most grotesque. When people saw me they laughed. Each train as it came up swelled the audience." Just as "St. Simeon Stylites" gives special comic force to Wilde's aphorism that "all martyrdoms seemed mean to the looker-on,"[5] so Tennyson contrasts deliberated endings with endings that cruelly parody the scripts a speaker writes for himself and painstakingly rehearses. Such ironies are themselves designed to dramatize what Wilde calls "the dreadful thing about modernity," the fact that it puts "Tragedy into the raiment of Comedy, so that the great realities [seem] commonplace or grotesque or lacking in style."[6]

After Tennyson's Simeon and Tithonus announce the proper ends for themselves in a drama of martyrdom and in an elegiac drama of relaxing into easy death, both speakers succumb, like Wilde, to another fate altogether, though one equally suited to the conventions of Ovidian comedy and metamorphosis. Tennyson displays his quietly ironic mastery of genres in the way he combines heroic and comic traditions. Neither monologue allows its speaker the luxury of matching what finally happens with the anticipated heroic way of describing and responding to it.

Chapter Nine
High Rhetoric and Plain Speaking: Tennyson's Heroines

Most of Tennyson's monologues by women display a wounded femininity, ambiguous because imagined by a man. The poet-ventriloquist's lips can be seen to move rhetorically and lyrically, so that behind both the high tone and plain speaking of Oenone, Demeter, Mariana, and the daughters of Hesperus we can hear Tennyson's own cadences and word music. Like Ovid, Tennyson poses as a public scribe to whom abandoned or jealous women have dictated their laments.

Mythical speakers like Oenone, Demeter, and the daughters of Hesperus are heroines in name only: the first two are passive but outspoken victims. And the third are cruel antiheroines, jealous guardians of fruit that, if shared with humanity, would heal the world's wound. Like Ovid's heroines, these mythical women might better be called women of the Heroic Age, famous (or infamous) females.

Unlike the moving film of Tennyson's stage plays and narrative poems, his heroines' monologues are snapshots or stills, poised upon some critical turning point in legend or myth. The readers may know that Mariana's patience will be rewarded by the return of the errant Angelo, as Penelope is rewarded by Ulysses' return in Homer and Ovid. Readers may also know that Hercules will steal the Hesperides' golden apples, despite their best efforts to guard them. But because the protagonists themselves can hardly guess these outcomes, the gaps between two levels of knowledge create small dramatic ironies in each poem.

Oenone is a more emancipated woman than the long-suffering Mariana, who, like Amelia Sedley or Caroline Helstone, is a familiar subject in Victorian social novels. The prophetic Oenone expands the range of female possibility by radically challenging the power structures governing her society. Why should vain goddesses like Aphrodite be allowed to subvert the institution of marriage by bribing Paris? Without questioning the need for marriage as society's main way of ordering desire, Oenone challenges the right of goddesses to sanction adultery and make it hard for a mere mortal like herself to find fulfillment as a wife.

Alternatively, strong-minded women may use silence to secure their
will. Though Aurora cannot make Tithonus her immortal consort, as a
silent auditor she has no problem manipulating silence to create an illusion of favor by smiling at him. In withholding her formal assent, Aurora
withholds part of herself. And in refusing to admit the full implications
of her smile, Aurora can always say she was too heartbroken, rather than
too cruel, to be wholly honest with Tithonus.

As outsiders, Tennyson's heroines struggle to become insiders. Except
for the long suffering Mariana in her "moated grange," they inhabit a
"free territory" or "wild zone," where overlooked gaps in the patriarchal
structure allow them to seize power. Paris's weak sensuality permits his
rejected wife to grow in stature by assuming the authority of Cassandra
and Dido, subverting traditional definitions of sexual identity. Rizpah is
a stronger character than her criminal son, and the Hesperides have
more power than Hanno. Though the rape of Proserpine becomes a
breeding ground of violence and hatred, Demeter's personality is just as
domineering as her son-in-law's. The unequal antagonism of Persephone
and her rapist-husband, Pluto, will be superseded, Demeter predicts, by
a new politics of sexual power, based on a consolidation of women's
interests against male tyranny.

By looking at herself as a pathetic spectacle, a picture of the betrayed
woman, Oenone views herself in Tennyson's monologue in the same self-
conscious way that her husband, Paris, views the three naked goddesses in
the beauty contest. Since men are conditioned to be voyeurs, they survey a
woman before they judge her. To gain control over the humiliation of
being looked at and possibly rejected like Pallas Athene and Hera, Oenone
contains and interiorizes the process. She acquires power by conniving in a
voyeur's treatment of her as, first and foremost, a spectacle or "sight."

> O mountain brooks,
> I am the daughter of a River-God,
> Hear me, for I will speak, and build up all
> My sorrow with my song, as yonder walls
> Rose slowly to a music slowly breathed,
> A cloud that gathered shape:
>   ("Oenone," ll.36–41)

As even sound effects are made visual, Oenone uses her powerful pictorial imagination to pass from dove-like lamentation: "My heart is

breaking, and my eyes are dim" (l.31) into powerful invocations and
petitions of decree: "Hear me, for I will speak" (l.38). "I will" is the auxiliary verb of volition, not to be confused with a weak use of the simple
future tense. To "build up" the harmony, she even allows her blank verse
to break into repetition ("Hear me," "hear me") and near-rhymes
(ll.38–39). But at the very moment we expect Oenone's striking shifts
from descriptive to performative speech to mount toward a climax, the
current of her feeling changes. The heavy overflow of the lines: "as yon-
der walls / Rose slowly" (ll.39–40) relaxes rather then braces the will.
And as the walls built to music give way to the even less substantial
image of the cloud gathering shape, the wave of rhythm seems to subside again instead of rising to its anticipated crest.

To bring into being what a lesser poet would merely describe,
Tennyson imitates Oenone's power to contain and recreate her world by
visualizing spatial effects through sound.

> She . . .
> Sang to the stillness, till the mountain-shade
> Sloped downward to her seat from the upper cliff.
> ("Oenone," ll.19–21)

The trough of weak syllables and the medial caesura make lines 20 and
21 slope down at their center, like a valley between two mountain sides,
in two miniature sound-portraits of their meaning.

The high rhetoric of Oenone, who is the "daughter of a River-God"
and speaks with a god's authority, turns at moments into the plain
speaking of a shepherdess, lovesick for her swain.

> Ah me, my mountain shepherd, that my arms
> Were wound about thee, and my hot lips prest
> Close, close to thine in that quick-falling dew
> Of fruitful kisses, thick as Autumn rains
> Flash in the pools of whirling Simois.
> ("Oenone," ll.198–202)

The tenderness and passion she babbles in these words seem wholly
unacted, as if she no longer aspires to speak or act the part of an epic
heroine. Her desire to swoon in her shepherd's arms, to draw her breath

in amorous pants, as the kisses come quick as falling dew, produce their own rapport with us. Not only is the phrase, a "dew / Of fruitful kisses," well confused, but in the grammatically ambiguous simile of the thick rains and flashing pools Tennyson also uses impressions of simultaneous weight and evanescence to complete the reinforcement of one sense by another.

The simplicity of Oenone's everyday words in everyday prose order is far removed from the simplicity of Wordsworth or Frost. Their artifice resides in the filtering of silver moon-lit clouds through narrow openings in the pine trees.

> Never, never more
> Shall lone Oenone see the morning mist
> Sweep through them [the pine trees]; never see them overlaid
> With narrow moon-lit slips of silver cloud,
> Between the loud stream and the trembling stars.
>
> ("Oenone," ll.211–15)

"Silver moonlight" would be hackneyed. But Oenone's sundering of the two impressions by the insertion of "slips" before "cloud" opens up discrete pictures in her mind. Harsh spondaic stresses make the "loud streams" sound clamorous, and even a wavering run of unstressed accents at the end of the passage manages to imitate the shimmering motions of the stars.

As tremulous with indecision as these stars, Oenone hovers between the childlike simplicity of her refrain: "O mother Ida, harken ere I die," and the high rhetoric demanded by her heroic performance as a wronged Dido or prophetic Cassandra. Whereas the Miltonic blank verse in "Ulysses" makes an epic impact on a reader, Oenone's more Keatsian blank verse induces slight shocks and aftershocks. Often tremors of feeling are created, as in Virgil's epic, by a casual aside or afterthought, or by a self-critical revision. By assimilating Oenone to Virgil's Dido: "aut videt aut vidisse putat" (*Aeneid* vi.454), so slight a trick of grammar as the casually inserted qualification: "and round her neck / Floated her hair or seemed to float in rest" (ll.17–18) introduces a tremor into the narrator's voice, even at one of Oenone's most poised and self-confident moments.

Because at the beginning of the monologue Oenone has not yet been humanized by her confrontation with the ruined vale of Ida, she cannot assimilate its meaning. To grow in stature she must learn to frame the ruined vale with past and present impressions of it. On one side is the apocalyptic imagination of a ruined universe, and on the other the pastoral imagination of a fostering nature. Their shared symbol is the ruined paradise, the devastated vale that stands between. Oenone is so stirred and bound by the spirit of place that it becomes at once her refuge and her prison. Hence there is potential victory as well as defeat in the destruction and derision she foresees and finally embraces. To exercise power Oenone even makes the distress of future events a feature of her own prophetic words, whose rhythm is wrecked by four successive stresses: "Lest their shrill happy laughter come to me" (l.254). To free her imagination from fixation on a specific place and to emerge from the blindness of fixed hope, Oenone, like her mother, the beautiful vale of Ida, finds that she has to be ravaged and despoiled before finding strength to grow.

Unlike Oenone and Demeter, the Hesperides are always intoning in a high rhetorical manner: as hierophants, they seldom speak plainly. One trouble with their monologue—and one reason why Tennyson may not have republished it during his lifetime—is that its intoxicating language is too obviously the work of a virtuoso poet, performing as a virtuoso. The Hesperides preside over ceremonial rites that deny life and breed death. When their words become genuinely riddling, they defeat rather than reward the intelligence that tries to make sense of them.

> If ye sing not, if ye make false measure,
> We shall lose eternal pleasure,
> Worth eternal want of rest;
> ("The Hesperides," ll.23–25)

So elliptical is the grammar that the Hesperides' meaning looks opposite ways at once. Is "their eternal pleasure" synonymous with their agitated state of watchfulness? Or is lethargy their pleasure? If so, they are in hell, because what they endure is the torment of perpetual activity and an "eternal *want* of rest."

The monologue reminds us of the etymological descent of "charm" from "carmen," a song, and of the capacity of a charm to lull the charmer asleep as well as achieve something magical with words. Like the distant sounds that Hanno hears as he travels along the African coast, the maze of monotonous murmur that a reader registers is often too muffled to be instantly intelligible. Indeed the exhortation to "watch, watch, ever and aye" (l.43) is teasingly at odds with the cadences of the falling dactyls and drowsy incantations. Nothing from the cyclical order of nature seems to enter this garden at death, and nothing proceeds into the world outside the garden at birth. Like Eden in Dante or the Garden of Adonis in Spenser, the garden is a place of seed and fruit. But the garden's "luscious fruitage" is ripened not by sun but by sunset, and its "Crocodiles in briny creeks" (l.21) recall Tennyson's hideous sea-dwelling kraken and other monsters.

Though the Hesperides are mythical versions of the Lady of Shalott and the female soul in the Palace of Art, their apparent power is only an illusion. Unlike the Lady of Shalott and the soul, however, who realize they are imprisoned and resolve to be free, the Hesperides celebrate their bondage. They use their words of power not to keep the dragons vigilant but to lull them asleep. The monologue is a remarkable example of the simultaneous use and evasion of a mythical *topos*: the prohibition against eating forbidden fruit.

Whereas the Hesperides are jealous and malign, lacking even the imagination of love, the animal source of Rizpah's love for her criminal son is at times more affecting than Demeter's more formal declarations of love for her daughter. Tennyson's use of octameter couplets, as in the dialect poems and "Locksley Hall," allows the madwoman to vent her ravings in a loose, indulgent meter. As life loosens its hold, the syntax unravels, and the long sixteen-syllable lines, fragmented by dashes, break into steadily diminishing units.

Nay—you can hear it yourself—it is coming—shaking the walls—
Willy—the moon's in a cloud—Good-night. I am going. He calls.
                                                    ("Rizpah," ll.85–86)

Two time sequences are confused in the mother's mind. She can hear her son calling to her at the time he was hanged in chains in order that all the passing ships could stare at him. On that occasion she had taken his bones down from the gibbet and buried them at night by the church-yard wall. But the mad mother can also hear his call to her at the hour of her death, when the chains are transferred from Willy's body to her own hands, chained now to her asylum bed. At moments the mad-woman inhabits both time frames simultaneously.

> Anything fallen again? nay—what was there left to fall?
> I have taken them home, I have numbered the bones, I have hidden
> them all.
>
> ("Rizpah," ll.9–10)

Although she is thinking of the bones that have fallen from the gibbet when she buried Willy, the mother is suspicious of her deathbed attendant, who has overheard what she says. With the cunning of the insane, she becomes secretive, pretending not to know what her repeated verb refers to: "Falls? what falls? who knows? As the tree falls so must it lie" (l.12).

Rizpah's vigorous performance of the madwoman's role is well within the conventions of Victorian melodrama. But like Edgar's acting the part of a mad beggar in *King Lear,* it can be overdone as a result. What saves the melodrama is the mother's elemental love, which holds fast forever and is beyond theater and playacting. The nightmarish naturalness of the mother's cherishing the bones she once nursed at her breast makes Willy's call to her natural, too: he is cold and lonely, a forsaken ghost, like the "infant crying in the night" in *In Memoriam* (54.18–20), "An infant crying for the light: / And with no language but a cry." Even when Willy is sucked into a hell of wailing winds and ghastly gibbets from a world of adventure games in which he robbed mail coaches to impress his boyhood friends, he is still simply her child, an object to be picked up and dandled, like the bones.

In the monologue of Tennyson's old age, "Demeter and Persephone," the high rhetoric acquires a touch of plainness and genuine mother-feeling only when the great earth goddess becomes a simple mourner, grieving in vain for her abducted daughter. When Demeter first uses the vocative of endearment, "Child" (l.23), she acknowledges that her formal mode of address may be deficient in motherly feeling, since she is still in awe of her daughter's "imperial disimpassioned eyes" (l.23), whose gaze is at once more and less than filial. Readers are moved by the contrast between official strength and individual weakness. In her conversation with her daughter, the mother does not at all aspire to speak and act the part of a deity. But not until she addresses Persephone as "Child" for a second time (l.51) can she abandon the stereotypes of heroic myth and babble out words of tenderness in envy of the simple pleasures of "human wives," "nested birds," and the lioness with her cubs (ll.51–53).

As Demeter grieves for the agony and strife of human hearts through grief for her missing child, she achieves a simplicity and plainness of speech that are more affecting than any of the solemn liturgies chanted in her temples.

> 'Where is my loved one ?' . . .
> I peered through tomb and cave, and in the storms
> Of Autumn swept across the city, and heard
> The murmur of their temples chanting me,
> Me, me, the desolate Mother! 'Where'?
>   ("Demeter and Persephone," ll.59–72)

Unlike the chanted rituals, even her triple turn upon the pronoun "me" is the opposite of rhetorical. "Desolate Mother" is a phrase that touches us deeply, because its revelation of a natural weakness contrasts with liturgical assertions of Demeter's strength and privilege as a goddess. As the weakness and vulnerability of both women blur distinctions between impotence and power, they bring mother and daughter into genuine intimacy for the first time.

Demeter acquires a gift of empathy, a capacity to take upon herself "the giant agony of the world," when she discovers that the earth is dark with grief and graves. Had Demeter not lost her daughter, she would not have been as sanctified through self-sacrifice and self-denial as thousands of mourners among her own worshippers. But now, the more impotent humanity becomes after jungles invade its shattered hearths, the more Demeter can empathize with suffering and be exalted through sympathetic identification with the pain and mystery of human life.

By grieving with her daughter and the rest of humanity Demeter comes to enjoy a secret and blasphemous superiority over the implacable Zeus, who is incapable of suffering with anyone. But Demeter can still not see that the burden of her empathy is also her greatest privilege. Instead, in promoting the primordial "serpent," "scorpion," and "tiger," like the "three gray heads" of the Fates (ll.76–78, 82), to the head of poetic lines, she momentarily forgets that the human mind is lord and master over outward sense. In the madness of a jumbled, upside-down world, the beloved daughter, who ought to be the crown and roof of things, is even demoted to lowly terminal position at the end of a line: "trace of thee / I saw not," her mother mourns (ll.79–80).

Hints of confusion and abortion point to the pervading impression of nescience in the monologue: "We know not, and we know not why we moan"; "We know not, for we spin the lives of men, / And not of Gods, and know not why we spin!" (ll.66, 84–85). Trapped in a world of "labyrinthine darkness" (l.81), Demeter loses herself in a maze without a plan. The muddledom and abuse of mind in this maze make her half crazed, a kind of mythological Rizpah. Nor is her bafflement appeased by the enigmatic disclosure that "The Bright one in the highest / Is brother of the Dark one in the lowest" (ll.93–94). The solemn absurdity of this oracle inspires Demeter's epic address to "the Gods of Heaven," whom she curses and then blackmails in lines that have their own sharply etched austerity and surrealist power:

> the leaf fell, and the Sun,
> Pale at my grief, drew down before his time
> Sickening, and Aetna kept her winter snow.
> ("Demeter and Persephone," ll.111–13)

Only when the monologue ends as a man might hope to die, do its subsiding rhythms combine with an enchanting vowel music to make "the dimly-glimmering lawns" (l.148) of the pagan elysium not the horror that Demeter earlier recoils from but a consummation devoutly to be wished. Since death is the mother of beauty, there seems to be something headstrong and perverse about Demeter's resolve to reverse for her daughter alone the doom reserved for all humanity. Who is Demeter to say that her daughter hates being queen of the underworld? Maybe she loves her husband and has no desire to live all year with Demeter.

The mother's furious rhetorical speeches owe half their terror to the presence of the stunned, silent daughter, who has no chance to restrain Demeter's embittered turbulence. If mother and daughter felt more comfortable in each other's presence, perhaps Demeter could express more by saying less. Tennyson's elegy for his son Lionel is a poetry of unvoiced apprehensions. Demeter, by contrast, seems guilty of a primal violation of family silence. She forgets that what a family feels it does not express, and that a mother's love, unless it verges on madness like Rizpah's, defeats the quality of acting.

Some of the most memorable moments in Tennyson's stage-plays allow the high rhetoric of politics and state to alternate with the simple pleas of a lover or a wife. As an English Oenone, Queen Mary feels deserted by Philip and pleads with him to remain in England one more day (V.i). Her argument from pathos, "And I am broken there," seems wholly unacted, as if the head of state had become suddenly a simple maid yearning for her lover. Philip's stern rebuke makes the queen's plain speaking particularly poignant.

> Do not seem so changed.
> Say go; but only say it lovingly.
> (*Queen Mary*, V.i, vol. 8, p. 171)

For once Mary sees the prince only as her husband, and the tenderness in her words seems wholly unrehearsed. Such trespass of sympathy is easier to achieve in history plays or political monologues than in epic narratives. Although Mary is the vampire of her people, Tennyson finds there is little room on stage for her enormous crimes, though space enough for her little graces. Whereas Mary's pleas with Philip to remain in England with her are babbled forth without premeditation, Philip speaks unfeelingly, with craft and calculation. Mary yearns to be a Tudor Cleopatra, whose heroic temper can never wholly disguise an endearing natural weakness. Philip, by contrast, is an Octavius Caesar: devoid of Antony's bounty, he embodies the politics without the passion of history.

Near the end of the play Mary becomes a child again, cutting her betrayer's picture from its frame, and then, in an infantile stupor, wailing she has killed him. It is also with a child's sense of comfort that she remembers her lover's counsel and takes to her death-bed.

> All is well then; rest—
> I will to rest; he said, I must have rest.
> (*Queen Mary*, V.v, vol. 8, p. 203)

Her decline into the plain speaking of a child playing games then seeking rest blurs distinctions between public strength and private weakness. Touched by a contrast between political rhetoric in full flow, scoring its points, and a plain, domestic way of speaking, we may feel uncomfortably closer to the queen than we want to feel.

Tennyson's heroines are more likely to shift from high rhetoric into plain speaking than his male characters. Queen Mary and the crazed Rizpah also exercise a power of charismatic illness or mania.[1] Even the Lady of Shalott perfects an art of protracted dying. Men are less skilled in these arts, perhaps because a man's best work is a result of what he *does,* and a woman's a result of what she *is.* Instead of becoming a star of slow decay and death, Tennyson's St. Simeon is a mere grotesque parody of such feminine counterparts as Browning's Pompilia or Tennyson's own Lady of Shalott.

There is a third difference between Tennyson's male and female characters. Lucretius is most revealing when his mind disintegrates and he inadvertently discloses the appalling pitfalls of his own philosophy. Similarly, we are never more intimate with Ulysses than when he loses his public identity and becomes, for a moment, his own audience—an observer of his future death at sea or of his encounter with Achilles in the underworld.

> It may be that the gulfs will wash us down:
> It may be we shall touch the Happy Isles,
> And see the great Achilles, whom we knew.
> ("Ulysses," ll.62–64)

By contrast, Oenone and Demeter acquire heroic status when they consolidate their public roles, either by prophesying disaster for their betrayers or by altering the outcome of events by blackmailing Zeus. Whereas male speakers become heroic when they collapse into intimacy by losing a grip on their public roles, heroines like Oenone and Demeter often maximize their prophetic authority by virtue of their specular power, their charismatic suffering, or their histrionic gifts.

Chapter Ten

Fox and Hallam on Tennyson: A Ventriloquized World

The discursive germ of Tennyson's plays is the statement: "I am Becket, and I confer on Becket all the powers of language he would possess were he Tennyson." A playwright's ability to become a character, and then make that character as eloquent as the playwright, is Shakespeare's peculiar gift. As an astonished D. H. Lawrence says, "When I read Shakespeare, I am struck with wonder / that such trivial people should muse and thunder / in such lovely language" ("When I read Shakespeare," ll.1–3). The discursive germ of Tennyson's dramatic monologues is a related but significantly different statement: "Dante's Ulysses appropriates me as a region of his consciousness. Such a legendary character speaks through me as a ghost speaks through a medium or a ventriloquist through a puppet." When Tennyson grows tired of Ulysses, he can raise a new ghost, lending a voice to Hamlet, whom Ulysses starts to echo in the fifth line: "That hoard, and sleep, and feed, and know not me." Such allusions create holes in the mask. Through such holes we can sometimes catch a glimpse of the poet or a master ventriloquist (call it God or a deeper level of Tennyson's own being, often associated with the unconscious) speaking through his conscious mind.

Because oblique glances are less likely than direct observations to disturb the objects being investigated, Tennyson often prefers to gaze through some obscure peephole of history by impersonating a dying Roman philosopher, an aged Homeric hero, or a betrayed wife pushed to the sidelines of her own life and history. Instead of recounting the judgment of Paris from the judge's point of view, Tennyson focuses on the off-stage reactions of his rejected wife, Oenone. In Dwight Culler's phrase, Tennyson is an "Alexandrian poet"[1] who seeks out neglected aspects of the famous Homeric stories in order to retell them from obscure new angles. In love with the remote corners and by-ways of history, the Alexandrian poet is literally eccentric in his off-center efforts to *reach* the center. But however intrigued Tennyson, like Ovid, may be by peripheral female points of view that dominantly male writers had tried to marginalize, he is not just a ventriloquist who speaks through the masks of characters in whom he risks being alienated. Though the poet is opaque to his characters, the characters are transparent to the poet.

Instead of impersonating a character in the manner of a playwright, becoming a Becket or Queen Mary and endowing that character with his own powers of language, Tennyson as a poet-ventriloquist reverses the process. He appropriates an historical or literary character, speaking through it as a ventriloquist might speak through a dummy. In monologues like "Oenone," "Mariana," "Ulysses," and "Demeter and Persephone," he does not so much bring a character to life as mimic a character already known to us in Shakespeare, Dante, or Greek mythology. To be more specific, he first mimics a forsaken woman, an ancient mariner, or a bereaved parent reunited with her daughter by assimilating the character to himself: in psychological language, he "introjects" the other. Then through a process of projective identification, the character who has first been transformed into a region of Tennyson's own mind is projected back upon the world as an externalized persona. This dramatized persona can never be alien to Tennyson, because as a projection of the inmost recesses of the poet's mind it is privy to his darkest secrets and imaginings.

The poet of dramatic lyrics and monologues no longer simply speaks through a persona. It is rather a question of the persona speaking through the poet. An old man determined to go on despite adversities addresses the young poet who has lost his best friend, Arthur Hallam. And a bereaved parent, Demeter, questioning God's providence, can speak more openly and bitterly than Tennyson, whose younger son, Lionel, has just died. Tennyson admits there is more of himself in "Ulysses" than in all of *In Memoriam*. And he is certainly freer to indict creation in "Demeter and Persephone" than in an intensely personal poem like his verse epistle to Dufferin, an elegy for Tennyson's dead son. The unforgettable power of the great classical monologue of Tennyson's old age resides in its stirring attack on Zeus, which seems deeply and frighteningly to implicate the poet at the moment he seems most secure, most removed from the tragedy of his young son's death.

The two parts of the process—introjection and projection—are ably described by Arthur Hallam and W. J. Fox, respectively, in their famous reviews of Tennyson's early poems. Hallam's poet of sensation assimilates to subtle shades of emotion in the poet's own consciousness objective correlatives of that emotion in the external world. He may seem to empathize with an actual literary character, as Tennyson empathizes with Ulysses, but only as a means of assimilating Ulysses' mental landscape to his own. Fox's poet is a transmigrating Vishnu who takes up residence in a host of alien selves, not because he has alienated himself in a foreign world but because that foreign world is itself projected from his mind. Tennyson can mimic and parody Simeon Stylites or the speaker in "Locksley Hall" because he knows them from inside.

In his influential theory of poetic empathy, published in 1831 in *The Englishman's Magazine,* Hallam praises poets of sensation like Tennyson, Keats, and Shelley for their remarkable ability to find in the "colours . . . sounds, and movements" of external nature, "unregarded by duller temperaments," the signature of "innumerable shades of fine emotion," which are too subtle for conceptual language to express.[2] In a *Westminster Review* article published earlier in 1831 on Tennyson's *Poems, Chiefly Lyrical* (1830), Fox argues that the poet can best concentrate his energies by sketching his relation to a desolate landscape or to some ruined paradise, as in Tennyson's "Mariana" or "Oenone." Tennyson, says Fox, "seems to obtain entrance into a mind as he would make his way into a landscape; he climbs the pineal gland as if it were a hill in the centre of the scene."[3] Every mood of the mind has its own outward world, or rather it fills the world with objects that the mind can inhabit. This insatiable Vishnu is Tennyson's version of the theatrical "star." Like Jean Davenport, the model for Dickens' Infant Phenomenon in *Nicholas Nickleby*, he is a prodigy of versatility. In his incorporative fantasies, the subjects whom Vishnu impersonates are also his life-blood, victims he becomes as well as feeds off, like Dracula. The poet of theatrical impersonation is a versatile vampire, living off the dead selves he becomes.

Precariously balanced between empathy and free projection, Fox's poet must perform a difficult high-wire act of the mind. On the one hand, his personality must be "modified" and even changed by the characters he becomes. He must be a "transmigrating Vishnu," in Fox's striking phrase, who can assume the nature of such "elemental beings as Syrens . . . mermen and mermaidens."[4] Unless he is open to the indignities of even the lowliest incarnations, Fox's Vishnu will be at best a sham ventriloquist, speaking through his puppets as a mere partisan or apologist. The true ventriloquist knows how to receive as well as give and is capable of taking back from his characters more than he is conscious of putting in.

On the other hand, the personality of the poet-ventriloquist can never be wholly "absorbed," Fox insists, by the puppets he creates.[5] Total absorption blurs an important distinction between the dramatized speaker's meaning and the poem's meaning, which is a defining feature of all Tennyson's monologues. Even in "Ulysses," there are ironic differences between the speaker's belief that "Death closes all" (l.51) and Tennyson's belief. Unless Fox's poet remains firmly in control of the licentious process of casting his spirit "into any living thing, real or imaginary," he degenerates into a moral cipher. Then the poet becomes a mere "poetical harlequin," a chameleon like Keats's poet of negative capability, who may gain the whole world yet lose his own soul.

In Tennyson's best dramatic poems we can hear behind each speaker the voice of the ventriloquist whose consciousness exceeds and spills over each mask that he wears. And behind the ventriloquist is a master ventriloquist, the "God" at the end of Tennyson's "The Vision of Sin," who makes "Himself an awful rose of dawn" (l.224). Tennyson seems to feel that if he descends deeply enough into the minds of Ulysses, Demeter, Oenone, and Lucretius, or even into the consciousness of the flower in the crannied wall, he will reach the unconscious or general mind, which is either an expanded version of his own mind or God's. Though Tennyson, like Keats's chameleon poet, attempts an arrogant self-effacement, his feeling for St. Simeon's strange tortures or for the grotesque anguish of Lucretius also expresses itself in what G. K. Chesterton calls "a desire after a kind of vagabond beneficence, a desire to go through the world scattering [goodness] like a . . . god."[6] Because even the spiritual confidence man, St. Simeon, or the atheist, Lucretius, may be a momentary incarnation of Fox's transmigrating Vishnu, we never know when the voice that comes through such an improbable mask will turn out to be an oracular voice, part of what Chesterton calls "God's everlasting soliloquy."[7]

Since each mask or object is also a false or distorting image of the consciousness that overflows it, a withholding speaker may be justified in his use of silence or reserve. At the end of "The Holy Grail," Arthur's puzzling summation, "Ye have seen what ye have seen" (l.915), leaves Percivale mystified. Tautology is the most withholding of tropes, because it allows a character to speak without saying anything. In "Tithonus" power resides with the actively silent auditor, the goddess of the dawn, whose silence holds consciousness like a sum of power in reserve. To have power is to have consciousness, and consciousness may express itself in silence as well as words.

The playwright of *Becket* and *Queen Mary* enters the minds of historical characters. But in the dramatic monologue Ulysses and Tithonus enter Tennyson's mind. The poet who raises legendary ghosts, like a medium at a historical séance, combines a talent for hearing voices with a ventriloquist's gift for projecting them. "To raise a ghost" by "commission[ing] forth" half the poet's soul may seem at first satanic. We think of Browning's zombie-like Lazarus, well suited after his resuscitation (perhaps by mesmerism) for a Victorian Chamber of Horrors. Resuscitating a corpse, however, need not be a form of Faust's black magic. It may be a benign act, a miracle of resurrection.

> ". . . then write my name with Faust's!"
> Oh, Faust, why Faust? Was not Elisha once?—
> Who bade them lay his staff on a corpse-face.
> (*The Ring and the Book,* I.759–61)

As in "Childe Roland," where the names of "lost adventurers" ring in the speaker's ears as they range like ghosts "along the hill-sides" (ll.195, 199), Tennyson discovers that when he conjures ghosts and then projects their voices, his communication with the dead Ulysses or Lucretius, far from giving off a whiff of the hoax or the charnel house, is tongued with fire beyond the language of the living. In conducting a séance at which readers may eavesdrop on the one-sided conversation of historical and legendary ghosts, the Tennyson who writes dramatic monologues is the channel of communication between the living and the dead: like Hallam or Christ, two other risen souls, he is the Way, and no one can come to the spirit world except through him.

PART THREE
Words of Power

Many admirers of Tennyson have experienced a conflict identified by Christopher Ricks: "the conflict between confidence in [the poet's] extraordinary expertise and faint uneasiness about the extent to which the expertise is . . . purely verbal."[1] To allay this uneasiness I want to show in the third section of the monograph that, despite Walter Bagehot's influential claim that Tennyson is merely an ornate poet, there are sources of fearful energy in his verse that make his poetry more sublime than ornate. Instead of merely dawdling with the painted shell of the universe, offering beautifully contrived descriptions, Tennyson's words of power bring into being sublime new meanings, even when, like Lucretius' words, they totter uneasily on the edge of hallucination or derangement.

Tennyson's ability to revise his poems, while leaving alternative conceptions to stand and to make creative use of his own self-borrowings, helps convert mere verbal refinement into an honesty and depth of personal statement that often astonish us. The double meanings that he holds in reserve and the resourceful use that he makes of poetic imitations and allusions allow Tennyson to impart to even his most conscious contrivances a surprising range of invention.

Chapter Eleven

Tennyson's Sublime: Apposition and Ellipsis

It was once assumed that Tennyson had a fine lyric gift, but that he had little except as an emotional poet to say. It was also assumed that he was an ornate poet, a Victorian beautician, deficient in powers of plain speech and directness. There is both an attraction and a danger to a single-minded theory about a poet's aptitudes. Though critics are always seeking a point of view from which their subject can appear in its greatest simplicity, in such matters it is also useful to recall A. N. Whitehead's injunction "to seek simplicity and distrust it."

It seems to me that the search for a simple interpretation of Tennyson is a trap that has too often snared his readers. I want to suggest at the outset that Walter Bagehot's well-known but simple-minded claim that Tennyson is an ornate poet[1] has done more damage to the poet's reputation than W. H. Auden's even better known but more outrageous charge that Tennyson is "the stupidest [English poet]; there was little about melancholia that he didn't know; there was little else that he did."[2] Though Tennyson's poetry may occasionally seem too ornate when compared with Wordsworth's mastery of a pure style or Browning's perfection of a grotesque one, I want to show that Tennyson is equally adept at beautiful and sublime forms of writing. It is innocuous enough to say that Tennyson is a stupid poet or a poet merely dedicated to fine-tuning the cadence and sounds of words, if one has never read him with care. What condemns the critic, as one commentator says, is "not the bias before the fair trial, but the bias that remains afterwards."[3]

Take as an example of Tennyson's beautifully ornate style the single magnificent sentence that crosses with ease three successive stanzaic breaks in section 86 of *In Memoriam*. The rare opulence is wholly functional, because it celebrates the power of sacramental landscapes to achieve a perfect equilibrium between the highly sensuous *forms* of nature—the "brake and bloom / And meadow"—and the "ambrosial air" that is breathed into these forms as their animating life force or *spirit*.

108 ALFRED LORD TENNYSON

Sweet after showers, ambrosial air,
    That rollest from the gorgeous gloom
    Of evening over brake and bloom
And meadow, slowly breathing bare

The round of space, and rapt below
    Through all the dewy-tasselled wood,
    And shadowing down the hornèd flood
In ripples, fan my brow and blow

The fever from my cheek, and sigh
    The full new life that feeds thy breath
    Throughout my frame, till Doubt and Death,
Ill brethren, let the fancy fly

From belt to belt of crimson seas
    On leagues of odour streaming far,
    To where in yonder orient star
A hundred spirits whisper "Peace."

                            (*In Memoriam*, 86.1–16)

The kernel of the sentence is "Air, fan my brows." But "air" is heavily
qualified by the clauses that come after, so that the mind has to double
back on the sequence that advances and returns upon itself in Virgil's
self-embedding manner. Grammatical elements that are conventionally
joined—the apostrophized "air" and the principal verb, "fan," for example—are disjoined to accommodate effects of marveling interjection.
The first line is generated by a conventional phrase, "sweet air," which
we recover by collapsing the *tmesis* that (in interpolating the modifiers
"after showers" and "ambrosial" between the first adjective and its noun)
is able to open up spaces in the mind. In the rest of the section the spaciousness is as much a function of the self-embedding syntax as it is of
the sacramental images or the expanding pattern of alliterating sounds
that help the poet cross gaping rifts between quatrains and lines.
    As the springtime landscapes bind the soul with obligation and affec-
tion, the closely huddled alliterating sounds at the beginning of the final

adverbial clause—"Doubt and Death," "fancy fly," "From belt to belt" (ll.11–13)—begin to disperse. The looser rhythm, without pauses we could clearly call caesuras, together with the looser sound patterning and the larger syntactic units, establishes a growing, relaxed movement, leading naturally into the harmony of the hundred spirits whispering "Peace." Unlike the bare diction of many of the elegy's earlier sections, the language is also ornate, beautifully befitting the dignity of a mind that can at last renew its world by achieving a perfect reciprocity between the landscape's animating breeze and its sensuous forms.

Such gorgeously decorative passages in Tennyson are often "beautiful" in a precise Hegelian sense. Hegel's important distinction between the beautiful and the sublime, which is familiar to readers of his posthumously published *Lectures on Aesthetics,* is important to grasp, because it was almost certainly known to Tennyson, who read Hegel in translation and owned a copy of his *Lectures on the Philosophy of History.* Hegel's theory of art, which influences the writings of the most ambitious of mid-century British critics, E. S. Dallas, and later the more famous Walter Pater, tries to explain how God *makes* or *constitutes* himself a grotesque animal god in ancient Egypt, then a beautiful human god in classical Greece, and finally the sublimely transcendent "I am that I am" of *Genesis*—or the equally sublime God-man of Christian faith.[4] Whereas the sublime Romantic art that Hegel equates primarily with music posits a disequilibrium between an increasingly attenuated sensuous form and a liberated spiritual content, struggling to free itself from matter, grotesque art of the ancient Symbolical phase, which Hegel associates mainly with architecture, reverses this ratio. It posits a disequilibrium between an attenuated spiritual content and that peculiar sense of material things—that power of tactile drubbing—which students of English poetry associate with Browning. True beauty, according to Hegel, is to be found in the Greek statues of the Classical period, which exhibit a perfect reciprocity of spiritual content and material form.

Beautiful in this strict Hegelian sense, because of its power to combine sensuous and religious ecstasy, is Tennyson's use of sacramental landscape in *Maud.*

> O, art thou sighing for Lebanon
> In the long breeze that streams to thy delicious East,
> Sighing for Lebanon,
> Dark cedar, though thy limbs have here increased,

Upon a pastoral slope as fair,
And looking to the South, and fed
With honeyed rain and delicate air,
And haunted by the starry head
Of her whose gentle will has changed my fate,
And made my life a perfumed altar-flame;
And over whom thy darkness must have spread
With such delight as theirs of old, thy great
Forefathers of the thornless garden, there
Shadowing the snow-limbed Eve from whom she came.
                                        (*Maud* I.613–26)

As the limbs of the tree increase, so do the lines' limbs, which ebb and
flow in an appreciative growth of wonder. The reader hears a reverent
voice, still vibrant after the crude ecstasy of the preceding lyric, but now
evaluative and analytic, cutting across the soaring tones and easy song.
Though the "merry play" (I.629) of the erotic stars, as they move "in
and out" among the swaying limbs, introduces a stroke of broad parody
across the solemnity of man's creation in the "thornless garden" (I.625),
the stars also form a beautiful bridal crown for Maud, who is both Eve
and Mary, the second Eve, the virgin of the *hortus conclusus* in the Song of
Songs. Indeed, so integral are the "delicate air" (I.619), the streaming
breezes (I.614), and the "starry head" (I.620) to a woman, a landscape,
and a biblical idea that without any straining for effect the lover uses
anaphora and protracted present participles to link a chain of grand
renewals. In his expansive description of a cedar of Lebanon tree, which
hovers between an ode and a psalm, much that pertains to sensuous and
spiritual mystery is implied.

Though Tennyson is a master of opulent biblical language, Bagehot's
claim that Tennyson is an ornate poet is just as wrongheaded as W. H.
Auden's less damaging because more absurd charge that Tennyson, a
writer of great emotional intelligence, is stupid. In fact, Tennyson's poetry,
like Wordsworth's, is far more memorable for its sublime effects than for
the felicitous beauty of the two passages I have just been analyzing.
Opulent verse is usually written in an expansive, appositional style. But to
establish Tennyson's mastery of sublime effects it will be necessary to look
briefly at his achievement in an elliptical as well as an appositional mode,
because he excels in both these forms of sublime writing.

A harrowing example of the expansive sublime occurs in the earlier passage in *Maud,* where the beloved's cold brilliance pulses in the northern sky like ghostly auroral light.

Cold and clear-cut face, why come you so cruelly meek

Passionless, pale, cold face, star-sweet on a gloom profound;
Womanlike, taking revenge too deep for a transient wrong
Done but in thought to your beauty, and ever as pale as before
Growing and fading and growing upon me without a sound,
Luminous, gemlike, ghostlike, deathlike, half the night long
Growing and fading and growing, till I could bear it no more,
But arose, and all by myself in my own dark garden ground,
Listening now to the tide in his broad-flung shipwrecking roar,
Now to the scream of a maddened beach dragged down by the wave,
Walked in a wintry wind by a ghastly glimmer, and found
The shining daffodil dead, and Orion low in his grave.

(Maud, I.88–101)

The passage is sublime because its auroral impressions of whiteness glimmering in "wintry wind" detach Maud from the Edenic grove of weird opulence and perfumed warmth in which the speaker finds himself. Yet the language is also expansive, using reversing metaphors to make light, colors, and forms flow together in a merging of cosmic and human elements. Orion "low in his grave" is also the poet's father, whose wail merges with the "scream" of a "maddened beach" (I.99); and the "shining daffodil dead" (I.101) is a precisely etched flower, seen against "the ghastly glimmer" with daylight accuracy.

The impressionistic blendings, which are just as often rhythmic as visual or aural, and the lack of strong pauses, increase marvelously the flowing movement and sense of pulsating growth. The expansive rise and fall of the ghastly light accompanies the surge of the hero's blood; and the series of magnificent rhythmic curves plunge downward and then upward, before culminating in the half-stormy sweep of "The shí / ning dáff / odil deád, // and Orí / on lów / in his gráve" (I.101). The recurrence of the same words and sounds, especially long arcs of adjectives of about the same size and shape—"passionless, pale, cold face" (I.91), "Luminous, gemlike, ghostlike, deathlike" (I.95), "broad-flung

shipwrecking roar" (I.98)—are wonderfully effective in expanding the
sense of circling flow.

A less expansive, more elliptical form of sublime writing can be found
in the same passage. As Maud is turned into the essence of the wintry
scene, a kind of northern nowhere connected with the eerie beauty of the
northern lights, she disappears momentarily behind dissolving syntax
and flickering sentiment. The syntax presents a parataxis of impressions:
terrifying beauty, focused in the phrase "cruelly meek"; heavenly splendor; fear converting wonder into self-defense; the sublimely transformed
avenger turning into a ghostlike apparition. The chains of epithets,
made remorseless by the repeated suffix ("gemlike, ghostlike, deathlike"—I.95), enact the pulsating glow, until growing and fading lights
begin to fluctuate in space like long-distance film shots. We are not to
imagine the lover hearing the roar of the sea, then looking at the shining
flower before gazing forlornly at the sinking star. We are meant to
receive instead, in a single mounting impression, something like
"seabeachmadness, wintrygleam, daffodil-stardeath."

When Tennyson starts experimenting with impressionistic syntax, he
finds it is only a short step from *Maud*'s expansive use of sublime language to the near abolition of syntax in that more frugal, elliptical use of
the sublime which is familiar to every reader of *In Memoriam*. In section
7 of the elegy, the "Dark house" and "Doors" are loosely joined to the
rest of the lyric by the expedient of turning these bare notations, the
most impersonal elements in the scene, into intimate apostrophes.

> Dark house, by which once more I stand
>   Here in the long unlovely street,
>   Doors, where my heart was used to beat
> So quickly, waiting for a hand,
>
> A hand that can be clasped no more—
>   Behold me, for I cannot sleep,
>   And like a guilty thing I creep
> At earliest morning to the door.
>
> He is not here; but far away
>   The noise of life begins again,

> And ghastly through the drizzling rain
> On the bald street breaks the blank day.
>   (*In Memoriam,* VII.1–12)

The hand and heart, the unlovely street and drizzling rain, begin to flicker disjointedly like film shots in a slow-speed movie; dissolving syntax gives a sense of emptiness and vertigo. As Alan Sinfield has noted, "Tennyson's sentence structure is moving in the direction of NO syntax,"[5] and the dissolution of grammar, even as it dissolves the mourner's world, also frees Hallam's spirit from the skeleton of an increasingly spare language, as Christ's is freed from the tomb: "He is not here; but far away" (VII.9). "This is great poetry," T. S. Eliot says, "economical of words, a universal emotion related to a particular place; and it gives me the shudder that I fail to get from anything in *Maud*."[6]

The most elliptically sublime moment in *In Memoriam* comes later, in section 123, where language contracts almost to the vanishing point. As in time-lapse photography, the contractions are so compressed—and the sequences so speeded up—that the mourner's emancipation of his soul from the world that dissolves around him is at first in danger of producing mere blackout and indifference, or even Pascal's fear of terrifying waste spaces.

> There rolls the deep where grew the tree.
>   O earth, what changes hast thou seen!
>   There where the long street roars, hath been
> The silence of the central sea.
>
> The hills are shadows, and they flow
>   From form to form, and nothing stands;
>   They melt like mist, the solid lands,
> Like clouds they shape themselves and go.
>
> But in my spirit will I dwell,
>   And dream my dream, and hold it true;
>   For though my lips may breathe adieu,
> I cannot think the thing farewell.
>   (*In Memoriam*, 123.1–12)

Here, if anywhere, we hear what Herbert Tucker has called "the ground swell of doom" in Tennyson's verse.[7] The imposition of the stern parataxis—"and they flow," "and nothing stands"—on the yielding similes—"like mist," "Like clouds"—establishes a momentary pathos. But the absolute parity of all the forms, of the moving and the motionless, of the gentle and remorseless, amounts to a sudden collapse in beauty and interest. The pageant seems about to end in terrifying absurdity, making the silence of Pascal's waste spaces seem by comparison like the pause between two movements of a sonata.

Even as the solid land seems to slide suddenly away into an indefinite void, however, there is still a resistance and a power in consciousness to save. By converting the most impalpable element, the dream of love, into the most palpable element, "the thing," the mourner shows how the more solitary his soul becomes, deserted by a dissolving earth, the more aware it becomes of its sublime power to survive the wreck of nature and create its own enduring world.

Occasionally the two sublime modes in *In Memoriam*, appositional and elliptical, come together in a single passage. In sections 54 to 56, for example, Tennyson uses anaphora, successive adjectival clauses, and run-ons between stanzas, all familiar features of the appositional sublime, to give man, God's noblest work, a spacious dwelling place in language.

And he, shall he,

Man, her last work, who seemed so fair,
  Such splendid purpose in his eyes,
  Who rolled the psalm to wintry skies,
Who built him fanes of fruitless prayer,

Who trusted God was love indeed
  And love Creation's final law—
  Though Nature, red in tooth and claw
With ravine, shrieked against his creed—

Who loved, who suffered countless ills,
  Who battled for the True, the Just,

> Be blown about the desert dust,
> Or sealed within the iron hills?
> *(In Memoriam, 56.8–20)*

The series of subordinate clauses modifying "Man" (l.9), which remains suspended for three stanzas without a verb, produces one of the most desperate moments in the elegy. The repetitive contrasts, accumulative doubts, and hysterical predicate of the quoted question mount in a crescendo of fear that is typical of the manic phase of depression and melancholia. The anxious insistence of the subordinate clauses brings the tempting slip into a frantic acceleration and tripling of the relative pronoun: "Who rolled . . . / Who built . . . / Who trusted" (ll.11–13); "Who loved, who suffered . . . / Who battled" (ll.17–18), as the grammatical subject tries frantically to detach itself from a world in which it feels increasingly estranged.

A moment later these expansive appositions collapse into word heaps that are barely grammatical. As the mourner elides the narrative of his own fearful depression, his grammar splits into syntactical fragments. Now he cannot even remember humanity's defining attributes, though in the earlier stanzas he seemed capable of remembering nothing else.

> No more? A monster then, a dream,
> A discord. Dragons of the prime,
> That tare each other in their slime,
> Were mellow music matched with him.
>
> O life as futile, then, as frail!
> O for thy voice to soothe and bless!
> What hope of answer, or redress?
> Behind the veil, behind the veil
> *(In Memoriam, 56.21–28)*

The final fearful decline into fragments without verbs—"No more? A monster then, a dream, / A discord" (ll.21–22)—wrecks the harmony of the "mellow music" (l.24). The section ends in a cacophony of disintegration, subsiding in the final breathless phrases, "Behind the veil, behind the veil" (l.28), to a momentary stasis of chord and discord, strained expectation and sharp distress.

Whereas the opening quatrains in section 95 of *In Memoriam* are elliptically sublime, the closing quatrains illustrate Tennyson's use of the
expansive sublime. Even before meanings are elided, the strongly
marked caesuras at the end of lines and clauses prepare for a slow contraction and silencing:

> For underfoot the herb was dry;
> And genial warmth; and o'er the sky
> The silvery haze of summer drawn;
> (*In Memoriam*, 95.2–4)

Is the silver haze of summer "drawn" over the nighttime sky, as a kind of
protective canopy or arch? Or is the silver haze momentarily drawn
back, as a curtain? Are we being shown something? Or is something
being concealed?

From the silence of the crickets' *not* chirping the mourner passes to
the distant sound of the brook, and then to the even less audible motions
of the flickering flame in the urn.

> . . . not a cricket chirred:
> The brook alone far-off was heard,
> And on the board the fluttering urn:
> (*In Memoriam*, 95.6–8)

Remote sounds, nonsounds, and eerie sounds of mere moving flame,
intimate the elusiveness of what Tennyson strains hardest to hear.
Though line 8—"And on the board the fluttering urn"—makes most
sense if an ellipsis of the passive verb "was heard" is assumed after "urn,"
the elliptical syntax heightens the strangeness and leaves the meanings
poised and hovering, on the quiver, as Hopkins would say. Some
neglected potency of language seems always on the point of escaping us,
slipping away through one of the caesural pauses, line breaks, or loosely
coupling "And"s.

Strikingly different are the incremental motions of the breeze in the
three concluding quatrains of section 95, which replace the contractions
of the elliptical mode with amplified repetitions.

> And sucked from out the distant gloom
>   A breeze began to tremble o'er
>   The large leaves of the sycamore,
> And fluctuate all the still perfume,
>
> And gathering freshlier overhead,
>   Rocked the full-foliaged elms, and swung
>   The heavy-folded rose, and flung
> The lilies to and fro, and said
>
> "The dawn, the dawn," and died away;
>   And East and West, without a breath,
>   Mixt their dim lights, like life and death,
> To broaden into boundless day.
>
> (In Memoriam, 95.53–64)

The short, monosyllabic verbs are the syntactic couplings, securely join-
ing the animated objects in nature to the supernatural breeze. With each
new stroke, the polysyndeton hammers the conjunctions into place:
"And fluctuate," "And gathering," "and swung," "and flung," "and said,"
"and died away," "And . . . mixt." The concentrated verbs combine with
the inventory of paired nouns to create simultaneous impressions of the
bounded and the boundless. As the flaring lights of East and West join
together to form a radiant center, Tennyson moves from natural obser-
vation to prophetic vision, yet so unobtrusively that we scarcely notice
what has happened.

Even at the elegy's expansive climax, however, the oblique elliptical
style that we thought the mourner had abandoned comes back to ravish
him and catch him off guard. The breeze that starts talking to Tennyson
is not the mighty wind that rocks the full-foliaged elm trees and that
builds up its energy incrementally, before turning into a kind of whirl-
wind or hurricane. Instead, the breeze that breathes the words "The
dawn, the dawn" is heard almost as a whisper, and just before it dies
away altogether. Nothing can translate these words. It is like walking on
silence.

Then Yahweh himself went by. Thence came a mighty wind, so strong it
tore the mountains and shattered the rocks before Yahweh. But Yahweh

was not in the wind. After the wind came an earthquake. But Yahweh was not in the earthquake. After the earthquake came a fire. But Yahweh was not in the fire. And after the fire came the sound of a gentle breeze. And when Elijah heard this, he covered his face with a cloak.

(1 *Kings* 19:11–13)

Like Elijah, Tennyson's mourner apprehends the sublime as a voiced silence, not as an impact but a tremor. At such a moment we experience the kind of calm vertigo that hurricane victims are said to feel when they find themselves at the still center of a storm and live to tell of their ordeal. To hear the breeze speak at all, the reader must linger with Tennyson's mourner over the breaks between caesural pauses and stanzas, listening there for the words that are otherwise inaudible.

Chapter Twelve

The Uses of Revision:
The Reinvented Poem

Tennyson's revisions take several forms: a poem can be so thoroughly rewritten that a poetic failure like the 1832 version of "The Lady of Shalott" emerges as a wholly successful lyric. By "re-viewing" a subject, creating two different versions of it, Tennyson also produces such companion pieces as "Nothing Will Die" and "All Things Will Die," modeled on Milton's "L'Allegro" and "Il Penseroso." But most interesting to critics are the reinvented poems that disclose a palimpsest of alternative poems beneath their surface. As Tennyson looks at a subject for a second or third time, he imposes new layers of meaning. Even in censoring what he once said, he allows traces of his original design to show through.

Helen Vendler uses the term "reinvented poem" to analyze the provisional quality of George Herbert's lyrics.[1] I want to show how Tennyson, like Herbert, welcomes the discipline of censoring his first thoughts, as an exercise in precision. Instead of rewriting these poems in private, as he does with the lyrics of 1832, he revises them in public, allowing Ulysses to substitute the more appreciative adjective "rugged" for the pejorative "savage" the second time he describes the Ithacans (ll.4, 37). The revised coda of "The Lotos-Eaters" leads us to expect a world-weary fadeout, as in the original ending. But Tennyson censors an escapist impulse by substituting for the shimmering dance motions of an uncritical celebration of the gods an angry indictment of them. The proper reading of "The Lotos-Eaters" must include both the tacit expectation and the implied rebuke. Similarly, when Tennyson's Lucretius commits a Freudian slip, admitting that his tongue trips or he speaks profanely, he has no leisure to cancel what he censors: he must let both the blasphemy and its correction stand.

In lays that will outlast thy Deity?

> "Deity? nay, thy worshippers. My tongue
> Trips, or I speak profanely.
> ("Lucretius," ll.72–74)

In "The Higher Pantheism" the most striking and memorable phrases allow us to trace Tennyson's reinvention of his meaning. When he praises "The sun, the moon, the stars" as "the Vision of Him who reigns" (ll.1–2), the phrase "of Him" is logically a subjective genitive. But Tennyson is not satisfied with an aloof emeritus deity who has retired from his creation. Without erasing his first sketch, Tennyson places a second picture over it. Turning the genitive from the subjective to objective form, he writes, "Is not the Vision He?" (l.3). If the world is the object of God's vision, how can the world itself be the envisioning God? And if God is defined as everything that lacks the power to feel "I am I," how can God also be defined as a "Spirit" with whom "Spirit can meet" (l.11)? Normally a poet who is critical of what he has written would remove all trace of his original misunderstandings. But Tennyson prefers to let the contradictions stand. His palimpsest of provisional sketches records his conviction that God's vision is not his own and that each renewed insight will disclose deeper contradictions. In Spinoza's biting phrase, a community of triangles would worship a triangular God, and Tennyson bends his mind to imagining what a better definition might be.

Reinventing his poetry as he writes, Tennyson discovers there is no traditional way of addressing God that he is not tempted to reject after being tricked into using it. Usually invoked by the masculine third-person pronoun, God is not just a "He" but also a "They," a "One" and an "All."

> That which we dare invoke to bless;
>   Our dearest faith; our ghastliest doubt;
>   He, They, One, All; within, without;
> The Power in darkness whom we guess;
>
> I found Him not in world or sun,
>   Or eagle's wing, or insect's eye;
>   Nor through the questions men may try,
> The petty cobwebs we have spun:
> (*In Memoriam* 124.1–8)

To compass the divine nature, Tennyson finds himself linking one attribute to another in a chain of contradictions. Refusing to remove the first links in his chain, he forges a sequence of paralogisms that read like footnotes to H. L. Mansel's riddling definitions of God in *The Limits of Religious Thought* (1858). Simultaneously personal and impersonal, singular and plural, ghostly and ghastly, God is both "Within" and "without" the human mind (*In Memoriam*, 124.3). As a ghostly conjurer, whose "dearest faith" is inseparable from his "ghastliest doubt," Tennyson is constrained to write his quatrain over, allowing successive contradictions to stand. As a "Power in darkness whom we [can merely] guess" (*In Memoriam*, 124.4), God possesses attributes that are inexpressible because inconceivable. Since he finds, like Kant, Sir William Hamilton, and H. L. Mansel, that he cannot univocally describe a subject that has no content in sense experience, Tennyson prefers to let several pictures of God succeed each other, untroubled by any discrepancies in his account.

The most marked and affecting moments in Tennyson's elegiac verse epistles to Fitzgerald and Dufferin come from a constant reinvention of the poet's way. His provisional conduct of each epistle reminds us of the necessarily provisional conduct of every life. Instead of censoring bleak thoughts about the deeper night, Tennyson recognizes reluctantly that he has reached that turning-point after which every milestone on his road is "a grave-stone," as F. H. Bradley says, "and the rest of life seems a continuance of [his] own funeral procession."[2] Fitzgerald's elegist looks inward, restoring life to clichés he has been tempted to use by envisaging the swift passage of the "full light / Of friendship . . . into darkness" (ll. 73–74) and his own dismal fellowship with the dead.

Similarly, the grieving father of the verse epistle to Dufferin makes no attempt to censor subversive thoughts about the comprehensive human wrongness of a son's dying before his father.

> To question, why
> The sons before the fathers die,
> Not mine! and I may meet him soon;
> ("To the Marquis of Dufferin
> and Ava," ll.46–48)

Even in rejecting his right to ask the question, Tennyson lets it stand, crying out for an answer. Though constantly criticizing what he has written, the mourner refuses to rescind his first thoughts. Instead, it is affecting that the question he both asks and does *not* ask should be allowed to show through, like a bone protruding through a wound.

Tennyson is a master of paraleipsis, the rhetorical trope that, in pretending to pass over a matter, tells it most effectively. His verse epistle to James Spedding introduces a paraleipsis similar to the asking of a question he refuses to ask in the lines to Dufferin: it repeats a platitude about death's being always at hand, which the reader is then asked to strike from the record and forget.

> I will not say, 'God's ordinance
> Of Death is blown in every wind;'
> For that is not a common chance
> That takes away a noble mind.
> ("To J. S.," ll.45–48)

"I will not say," the poet says, even as he says it. So eager is he to have his first thoughts about death conform to his own corrected notions that he admits a moment later: "I wrote I know not what" (l.57). If Tennyson now rejects a cliché he once received and embraced, why does he not revise his quatrain before allowing it to assume its final form?

He allows his self-correction to stand, I think, because, as the signature of his self-divided mind, it sanctions other uses of two-way meaning in the elegy: "Lie still, dry dust, secure of change" (l.76). Is the dead Edward Spedding assured of change, secure in the knowledge that nothing is immune to change but change itself? Or is he now protected from change? Is he as secure in his grave as a prisoner in his cell, on whom a secure lock bolt has been turned? Tennyson's changes of mind in an attempt to exercise his affections and be emotionally precise allow him, like Penelope, to undo what he does, unraveling his thoughts even as he pieces them together.

At other times it is hard to tell whether Tennyson is reinventing his poems' logic and grammar, or is simply betraying the expectations of an uninventive reader, whose mind runs on one track only. In sections 7 and 86 of *In Memoriam* the first quatrains seem to describe the bleak house in Wimpole Street and the springtime landscapes that bind the mourner's soul with obligation and affection. But when we finally arrive at the deferred principal verbs, we discover that the petitions to the door to "Behold" the mourner and to the "air" to "fan" his brows have unexpectedly substituted performative for descriptive speech. Objects or elements that we thought were merely being described have to be resuscitated like corpses. As apostrophized powers and presences, they enjoy a resilient posthumous life.

By inviting us to misconstrue his grammar, Tennyson is in effect rewriting *In Memoriam* with his usual precision. He is flashing before our minds two successive pictures: one of an inanimate world outside the mourner's mind, which the poet can only mirror passively, and the other of an animated world in which the prayerful poet is the most important agent, a lord and master over outward sense.

In other poems the flicker of incongruous pictures is so speeded up as to seem almost instantaneous. The disparate pictures that Ulysses mounts in his spacious line, "Far on the ringing plains of windy Troy" (l.17) is more like the montage in a cinema than a sequence of reinvented portraits. Ulysses' quick re-vision of Troy is a kind of "double-take," combining subliminal impressions of "ringing plains," alive with the clamor of war, and empty windswept ruins. By presenting separate pictures of battle on the darkling plain and of Troy as the bare ruined choir of wasting winds, Ulysses collapses the space filled by years of conflict into a direct confrontation of pride and ruin. Refusing to revise his boldly disparate impressions, Ulysses tries to do justice to both the devastation and the glory. To this end the multiple metonymies that speed his mind allow it to cross enormous intervals of space and time. Equally speeded up are the shocking pictures of hills as shadows, and of solid lands as mist, that Tennyson's mourner manages to run together in section 123 of *In Memoriam*, as if he had just taken a time-lapse photograph of the earth extending over billions of years.

Like his Ancient Sage, Tennyson records that since early boyhood silent repetitions of his proper name allow him to pass "into the Nameless, as a cloud / Melts into heaven" ("The Ancient Sage," ll.233–34). Sometimes the dazed repetition of contradictory phrases, which we might expect a more logical poet to revise or censor, functions as just such a mantra. In his elegy for Sir John Simeon, "In the Garden at Swainston," for example, Tennyson uses mantra-like phrases to induce stupor or trance.

Nightingales sang in his woods:
   The Master was far away:
Nightingales warbled and sang

Of a passion that lasts but a day;
Still in the house in his coffin the Prince of courtesy lay.

Two dead men have I known
  In courtesy like to thee:
Two dead men have I loved
  With a love that ever will be:
Three dead men have I loved and thou art last of the three.
                    ("In the Garden at Swainston," ll.6–15)

Though the tremor of open vowels sounds as resonant as the nightingales' "high requiem," the celebratory impulse is held in check by the stupefying numbness. If the mourner has literally loved the dead Simeon as he has loved two other "dead men" "With a love that ever will be" (l.14), why does he continue to say "Two dead men" instead of "Three"?

If the mistake is merely the result of an ellipsis, then we may interpret Tennyson to mean that, just as he has known only two other men who were as courteous as Simeon, so he has known only two others—Hallam and Henry Lushington—whom he loved so well. But though that may be his meaning, it is not what he says. Instead, there is a startling lack of censorship in the lines. In showing his willingness to say how things are, choosing the accurate phrase, and following the truth of feeling where it leads, Tennyson appears to be saying that the lasting love he feels for Hallam and Lushington does not include Simeon. He has loved "three dead men," but only the first two of them "With a love that will ever be." Precision is important, and instead of correcting an error in counting, Tennyson invites us to re-invent his meaning. Refusing to force his praise beyond the limits of an imperfect sympathy, the elegist is searching for the exact and honest tribute.

In the final line of the elegy the mourner seems to count correctly, but not without superimposing two more discrepant pictures: "Three dead men have I loved and thou art last of the three" (l.15). Does the elegist mean simply that Simeon is the most recent of his friends to die? Or does he mean, more devastatingly, that as the last of the courteous friends he has loved, Simeon is the last person he will be able to write an elegy for?

The odd blend of scenarios, which permit successive but contradictory dramatizations of the poet's deathward decline, confirms James Richardson's judgment: "Tennyson is a poet of deep inarticulateness, but he is an *emotional* intelligence of the highest order."[3] The elegy for Simeon shows Tennyson's honesty and care in charting the exact truth of his feelings—a much harder task, as George Eliot recognizes, "than to say something fine about them which is *not* the exact truth."[4] Though the stupor or numbness of Tennyson's refrains comes from the removal, not merely of Simeon, but also of any clear indication of what tone is to be elicited from successive reinventions of his meaning, "the vagueness is where Tennyson is most precise." As Richardson concludes, "we should not, in the large gestures of his language, lose sight of his essential emotional accuracy."[5]

A mantra-like refrain can convey a great deal to Tennyson, precisely because it seems to say nothing. Though his reinvented poems often consist of pauses filled by words, they are poems of unvoiced meaning rather than of mere blank intervals. Like Flaubert's association of the parrot with the Holy Ghost, the poet's mute obsessions show how almost anything from a flower in a crannied wall to a mantra-like repetition of a proper name can be given a sacred function. Contradictory or meaningless lines, which other poets might be tempted to amend or revise, may throw over an apparently trite or empty phrase the halo of the sacred. Tennyson values these words and objects, not because they are all equally holy but because they are all equally indifferent. A "terrible beauty" attaches to the flower and the repeated proper name, not because they *represent* a class of special things, but because they *present* the special class of sacred objects. Their purity would be less inviolable if it were not so arbitrary.

In "Tears, Idle Tears," the more Tennyson turns a word over, scrutinizing it from all sides, the more it defeats his understanding: "Tears, idle tears, I know not what they mean." But by the time Tennyson has taken his detour through the lyric's cycle of similes—"Fresh as, . . . Sad as" (ll.26–28), "sad and strange as" (l.31), the contradictory attributes of "the days that are no more" (l.30) have come to life with an unanticipated immediacy and precision. The vagueness and confusion of the one picture soon become the minute, topographical scrutiny of the other. If Tennyson is awed by the vastness of "the underworld" (l.27) and the strangeness of "dark summer dawns" (l.31), he is equally stirred, like Pope and Virgil, by an exquisite sense of the beauty in microcosms, by the charm of the "first beam glittering on a sail" (l.26) or "The earliest pipe of half-awakened birds" (l.32). By the time we reach the end of the lyric we have a very clear sense of what Tennyson means by the freshness and sadness of "the days that are no more."

And yet instead of revising anything, Tennyson allows his initial confusions to stand. He prefers to remain in a state of reversible equilibrium
between comprehension and incomprehension, subdued elation and
despair. By carefully reinventing his lyric, allowing contradictory impressions to remain, he also places himself between objects that are present
and objects that are vanishing; between the *presence* of such formal elements as oxymoron or anaphora and the *absence* of rhyme; between
everything that is intelligible in the present internal moment and everything that is unintelligible, forever beyond it in space or time.

Because the poet's flagging pulses can scarcely sustain the metrical
pulse to the end of a line, no poem in the world comes so close to being a
sob as "Break, break, break."

> Break, break, break,
>   On thy cold gray stones, O Sea!
> And I would that my tongue could utter
>   The thoughts that arise in me.
>   ("Break, break, break," ll.1–4)

Surprising the reader by discounting his power to say what he feels,
Tennyson seeks distraction in the innocent pleasures of "the fisherman's
boy" (l.5), the carefree toil of the "sailor lad" (l.7), and the progress of
the ships. The silence of the grave finds the poet mocked by the change
of contour, as the desolate scene yields to more buoyant and stately
impressions at the center. After taking a detour around his real subject,
however (the "thoughts" that he says his "tongue" cannot "utter"), he
finally finds the power to utter them: "But O for the touch of a vanished
hand, / And the sound of a voice that is still!" (ll.11–12).

Having reinvented his lyric, we might expect that Tennyson can now
revise or rescind the bleak austerity of the opening lines. Instead, he
allows both pictures to stand, as if he were setting at war two discordant
versions of his world. The final quatrain repeats the lyric's opening line;
and weighted with monotony, it discovers the same loss everywhere:

> Break, break, break,
>   At the foot of thy crags, O sea!
> But the tender grace of a day that is dead
>   Will never come back to me.
>   ("Break, break, break," ll.13–16)

Just when the elegist seems to have rewritten his poem, he allows the original despondency to return. Both pairs of lines stand like epitaphs, in strict grammatical autonomy; and the second pair, the most desolate of them, is an epitaph for the mourner. Though there is no escaping the powerful barrenness of the refrain, the lyric is redundant in circling back obsessively to its bleak impressions of loss. Two discrepant pictures are allowed to remain, without any effort to adjust them.

In several lyrics of *In Memoriam* the picture in the mourner's mind fails to match the picture before his eye. But instead of resolving contradictory impressions in one coherent attitude, each picture is allowed to trace the path of different feelings. In section 101, for example, where Tennyson anticipates a scene of neglect and oblivion after his family leaves Somersby and the garden-boughs and flowers fall into ruin, the picture of an estranged place, "familiar to the stranger's child" but unfamiliar to Tennyson, refuses to connect with the pastoral picture before his eye of sunflowers and babbling brooks. Instead of trying to adjust the two pictures by revising his first impressions, Tennyson reinforces the discrepancy by moving the negative past passive participles—"Unwatched," "Unloved," "Uncared for"—to the head of successive stanzas.

> Unwatched, the garden bough shall sway,
>   The tender blossom flutter down,
>   Unloved, that beech will gather brown,
> The maple burn itself away;
>
> Unloved, the sun-flower, shining fair,
>   Ray round with flames her disk of seed,
>   And many a rose-carnation feed
> With summer spice the humming air;
>
> Unloved, by many a sandy bar,
>   The brook shall babble down the plain,
>   At noon or when the lesser wain
> Is twisting round the polar star;
>
> Uncared for, gird the windy grove,
>   And flood the haunts of hern and crake;

> Or into silver arrows break
> The sailing moon in creek and cove;
>   (*In Memoriam*, CI.1–16)

As the quatrains unfold, however, each negative impression is tacitly rebuked. For the power of these negative participles depends, in one critic's words, "on the unsaying of the very detail" they seem to present.[6] "Unloved," the repeated negatives at the head of lines insist on saying. But also "loved," and deeply so, by the elegist who discovers, with a slight tremor of elation, that no mirror of place, however bleak, can be unhinged from the memorial of a self-conscious mind. The placement of one picture over another creates what James Richardson calls "a palimpsest, a dimness" in this reinvented lyric. "No," the reiterated impressions of loss keep saying, but also "yes." Because "Tennyson's simplest and most profound delight in language is with its ability to say yes and no at the same time,"[7] he finds he can best remember Somersby when he seems to forget it.

Tennyson's impulse to scrutinize and be critical coexists in section 10 with a readiness to begin a lyric with a trite account of foreign travelers and of a sailor returning to domestic comforts. Over the safe, the bland, the familiar, however, he places impressions of a more disturbing kind.

> Thou bring'st the sailor to his wife,
>   And travelled men from foreign lands;
>   And letters unto trembling hands;
> And, thy dark freight, a vanished life.
>   (*In Memoriam*, X.5–8)

A letter received with "trembling hands" is probably no ordinary letter. And the "dark freight" of a "vanished life" has power to alarm and unnerve the reader, perhaps because it is a conceit that defeats the understanding, a paradox that is only half intelligible. As a fictional character explains in A. S. Byatt's novella "The Conjugial Angel," "the *weight* of the freight, so to speak, is the weight of absence, of what is vanished, a lost life. It is not what remains that is heavy, but what is not there."[8]

Like the lyric's bland beginning, the overwrought periphrasis of the "kneeling hamlet" draining "The chalice of the grapes of God" cloaks the truth in a pall. But as the "hands" that used to clasp Tennyson's are imagined to "toss with tangle and with shells," fathom-deep in brine, like the corpse of the drowned Lycidas, honesty impels the elegist to reinvent and amend his deceptively soothing first impressions. Though he does not cancel his pastoral thoughts, the consoling picture of the dead man resting beneath "the clover sod" soon becomes the submarine nightmare of the corpse engulfed by "roaring wells."

> I hear the noise about thy keel;
>
> . . . .
>
>   O, to us,
> The fools of habit, sweeter seems
>
> To rest beneath the clover sod,
>   That takes the sunshine and the rains,
>   Or where the kneeling hamlet drains
> The chalice of the grapes of God;
>
> Than if with thee the roaring wells
>   Should gulf him fathom-deep in brine;
>   And hands so often clasped in mine,
> Should toss with tangle and with shells.
>   (*In Memoriam*, X.11.1–20)

By allowing the picture of burial at sea to correct the unreal pastoral picture, Tennyson can repudiate his own dishonest ornateness, moving with ease between alternative scenarios. Under the unsparing review, the whole disturbing truth about drowned corpses and burial ships comes into focus for the mourner. Instead of erasing his earlier picture of an unreal paradise, Tennyson allows his first, less accurate impression to show through. To dramatize the swift progression in honesty and intimacy, he finds that like Wordsworth in "Elegiac Stanzas" he must register both his fond illusions and his sobering corrections, his blindness and his insight, the thoughts he voices and the more affecting and disturbing ones he often leaves unsaid.

Chapter Thirteen

Dramas for the Eye and Ear: Speech at Odds with Lyric Form

Sometimes the counterpointed meanings that are available only in a silent reading of Tennyson's poems create a polyphony that allows him to speak with a divided mind upon a subject. When odd assortments of sense and sound in the revised coda of "The Lotos-Eaters," for example, send a reader in search of its silent or unspoken meanings, the interplay between the figures of rhetoric or rhyme that we *see* on the printed page (*opsis*) and the rant that we *hear* in the speaking voice elicted from the printed words (*melos*) creates a drama for both eye and ear that would be unavailable in an oral recitation alone.

Let us swear an oath, and keep it with an equal mind,
In the hollow Lotos-land to live and lie reclined
On the hills like Gods together, careless of mankind.
For they lie beside their nectar, and the bolts are hurled
Far below them in the valleys, and the clouds are lightly curled
Round their golden houses, girdled with the gleaming world:
Where they smile in secret, looking over wasted lands,
Blight and famine, plague and earthquake, roaring deeps and
  fiery sands,
Clanging fights, and flaming towns, and sinking ships, and praying
  hands.
But they smile, they find a music centred in a doleful song
Steaming up, a lamentation and an ancient tale of wrong,
Like a tale of little meaning though the words are strong;
Chanted from an ill-used race of men that cleave the soil,
Sow the seed, and reap the harvest with enduring toil,
Storing yearly little dues of wheat, and wine and oil;
Till they perish and they suffer—some, 'tis whispered—down in hell

Suffer endless anguish, others in Elysian valleys dwell,
Resting weary limbs at last on beds of asphodel.
Surely, surely, slumber is more sweet than toil, the shore
Than labour in the deep mid-ocean, wind and wave and oar;
Oh rest ye, brother mariners, we will not wander more.
                              ("The Lotos-Eaters," ll.153–73)

There is a wild abandon at the center of the speech, a sense of vastness, created in part by the volleys of triple rhymes, by the spacious inventories, and by the patterns of diverging alliteration. This expansiveness contrasts dramatically with the sudden shrinking and constriction of the grammatical units in the last two lines. The contraction is reinforced by the convergence of alliterating consonants, especially of the widely spaced "r" sounds in "Oh rest ye, brother mariners," which come together in the final phrase, "we will not wander more."

The expansion and contraction of alliterating sounds and converging triple rhymes are features of *opsis* rather than *melos*. As we *see* the long lines sprawl out spatially on the printed page, arranging themselves into heavily end-stopped units of triple rhymes, we sense that the mariners are too aroused and angry to subside into lethargy. Like their inquisition of the gods, the prospects of life on the high seas, beyond the shores of lotos-land, are also magnificently bracing and invigorating, whatever the mariners may say to the contrary.

In a silent reading of the coda the rant that is in danger of overpowering any oral recitation will begin to split up into a variety of more nuanced tones. Power-hungry bluster will prevail only so long as the lotos-eaters continue to identify with the gods. At some point in their long epic simile, we must imagine the figures of rhetoric and rhyme beginning to change the tone of voice, first into a world-weary rejection of the calamities from which the lotos-eaters flee, but then into something altogether more blasphemous and heroic: a sustained indictment of creation. It will be difficult for a good actor to dramatize these shifts in an oral recitation. Only in the privacy of a silent reading can the patterns of alliteration and the expanding and contracting rhymes on the printed page be *seen* to create in the suspended epic simile a liberating option for the lotos-eaters.

In striking contrast to the shimmering dance motions of the original ending, the lotos-eaters now seem too agitated to stay in lotos-land. As the skewing of the energetic sounds and the enervated pastoral sense sends us in search of a hidden meaning, the long epic simile combines with a striking shift in rhythm and line-length to dramatize the main irony in the coda. In their simile the mariners do not come out where they intended, and it is clear from the beginning that they will not remain in lotos-land, as they have planned. Or perhaps we should say that the presence of Ulysses, whose staccato voice rings throughout the poem: "'Courage!' he said, and pointed toward the land" (l.1), inspires the mariners to stirring insights they did not have before they started speaking. As one critic says, "to say we think first and then speak is a false metalepsis, a reversal of the true order of cause and effect."[1]

Initially identifying with the cruel epicurean deities, the mariners, by the end of their simile, have come to oppose everything the gods stand for. The self-pity of the gods' long-suffering victims and the aroused anger of plaintiffs, launching their denunciation of injustice, clash dramatically. And yet the emotions are allowed to pull apart only so they can come together and work in harmony again at the level of the subtext, which is the level of the poem's silent or unspoken meanings.

Counterpointing against hypnotic song a self-critical, protesting tone that presses ahead across the grammatical breaks, using cumulative syntax to produce effects that are at least as visual as they are aural, the impulse to turn blasphemy into a heroic enterprise is allowed to swell out the line lengths and rhymes, acquiring a touch of Lucretian grandeur. In creating one drama for the eye and another for the ear, one story about Promethean heroes conducting their cosmic inquisitions and another story about self-absorbed escapists (Greek versions of the Byronic ranter in "Locksley Hall"), Tennyson intimates that the mariners will leave lotos-land, not because they are too weak to keep their oath, but because they are too strong. The desire to become pleasure-seeking aesthetes is unworthy of them.

In *Enoch Arden,* as in "The Lotos-Eaters," lush descriptions of the mariner's tropical paradise allow dramas to emerge on the printed page that would easily be lost in an oral recitation.

> the glows
> And glories of the broad belt of the world,
> All these he saw; but what he fain had seen
> He could not see, the kindly human face,
> Nor ever hear a kindly voice, but heard
> The myriad shriek of wheeling ocean-fowl,

> The league-long roller thundering on the reef,
> The moving whisper of huge trees that branched
> And blossomed in the zenith, or the sweep
> Of some precipitous rivulet to the wave,
> As down the shore he ranged, or all day long
> Sat often in the seaward-gazing gorge,
> A shipwrecked sailor, waiting for a sail.
>
>   (*Enoch Arden*, ll.574–86)

Unable to hear a kindly voice, Enoch is troubled like the reader by an odd relation to his own voice. In a silent reading the lavish anaphora, word lists, and appositional phrases create abundant sensations for the eye that are missing for the ear. For despite the aural impressions, the "myriad shriek of wheeling ocean-fowl" and the thunder of the wave breaking on the reef, the ear, which is the organ of sense most in touch with Enoch's feelings, is still denied a listener. Perhaps this is why, like Coleridge in "Dejection: An Ode," we "see, not feel, how beautiful" this paradise is (l.38).

A recitation of the lushly extravagant passage I have just quoted would be less effective than a silent reading, because it would be in danger of reducing its tropical violence of taste to a mental gaudiness and monotone. By contrast, a silent reading can make the waters glow and the island blaze up for the eye with sudden interest, even as it can dramatize the dull anaphoric shape these same impressions may assume in the absence of an auditor.

> The blaze upon the waters to the east;
> The blaze upon his island overhead;
> The blaze upon the waters to the west;
> Then the great stars that globed themselves in Heaven.
>
>   (*Enoch Arden*, ll.590–93)

The passage's sound is more oppressive than its tenor, whereas on the page the merely potential monotony also has an air of intense scrutiny about it. As Enoch keeps scanning the horizon for a sail, his longing and alertness to any sign of change allow him beautifully to imagine how a shipwrecked mariner might wish to speak out loud about his tropical home, if only some companionable auditor were present to play Friday to his Crusoe.

As in *Enoch Arden,* a silent reading of the coda of "Demeter and Persephone" elicits from the printed page a drama for both eye and ear that would not be available in an oral recitation.

> and see no more
> The Stone, the Wheel, the dimly-glimmering lawns
> Of that Elysium, all the hateful fires
> Of torment, and the shadowy warrior glide
> Along the silent field of Asphodel.
>
> (ll.147–51)

"And see no more," Demeter says prophetically. But we do see more. Not only are we given an unforgettable glimpse of the Virgilian under-world, but we also see how the expansive modifiers and tenseless infinitives defer closure spatially on the printed page, as the lines wind down to their appointed end with as reluctant and unhurried a conclusion as any poem can have.

As the coda focuses, with full pathos, on "the Stone," "the Wheel," and the "field of Asphodel," the prophetic certitude of "see no more" is quietly discarded. Demeter says one thing, but the printed page allows us to see how the spacious run-ons and anaphora defy closure by muting the force of the line-breaks until we reach the final end-stopped line. Only in a silent reading can we see how slowly Achilles moves in the last great lines, and how twilight descends the way a man might hope to die.

In lyric 121 of *In Memoriam,* no vocalization of a phrase like "a glory done" can achieve what a silent reading does. A skilled reader would have to opt for either "a glory *done*" or "a *glory* done," since it is impossible to give both inflections simultaneously. Only in the privacy of a silent reading is it possible to preserve the vocal ambiguity that allows the mourner to look both directions at once.

> Sad Hesper o'er the buried sun
> And ready, thou, to die with him,
> Thou watchest all things ever dim
> And dimmer, and a glory done:
> (*In Memoriam,* 121.1–4)

Such physical features of the printed words as the shrinking space between "him," "dim," and "dimmer" show how the burial of the sun contracts the verse spatially. At the same time the ellipses—"Sad Hesper o'er," and "all things ever dim / And dimmer"—pull readers in the opposite direction by inviting them to open up spaces in the grammar that the compressed two-way meanings close and seal off.

As in *In Memoriam,* only a silent reading of the lyric "Break, break, break" allows us to see how the mourner's voice breaks on the page against the hard edge of print.

> Break, break, break,
> On thy cold gray stones, O Sea!
> (ll.1–2)

> Break, break, break,
> At the foot of thy crags, O Sea!
> (ll.13–14)

The incisive caesural breaks between the words "Break, break, break" are a form of "doing-by-saying," a means of *using* as well as *mentioning* the idea of breaking.

> And I would that my tongue could utter
> The thoughts that arise is me.
> (ll.3–4)

> But the tender grace of a day that is dead
> Will never come back to me.
> (ll.15–16)

Crossing the line breaks after "utter" and "dead," the heartbroken poet also allows us to visualize his consolation as two spacious run-ons. After the short one- and two-word units that precede these run-ons, where the incisive caesural breaks are experienced as a form of breakdown or breakup, the eye can now register the crossing of the line breaks as a minor breakthrough instead.

Whereas Tennyson's lyrics explore the feelings of a mind in conflict, the poems that he writes for choral recitation versify a patriotic doctrine or creed. Published with music and written for a choir of four thousand voices, the harmony of word and sound in Tennyson's "Ode Sung at the

Opening of the International Exhibition" appropriately looks forward to
a union of men in "noble brotherhood" (l.38). The commercial exchange
and goodwill promoted by an international exposition are not to be confused, however, with Tennyson's old dream of a "Parliament of man, the
Federation of the world" ("Locksley Hall," l.128). When Tennyson finds
himself drifting into overeasy optimism, he pulls himself up sharply: "Is
the goal so far away? / Far, how far no tongue can say, / Let us dream our
dream today" (ll.29–31). Though second thoughts and reservations
abound in Tennsyon's ceremonial poems, the ode's setting of words to
music cannot explore them fully. As a triumph of ingenuity, like the
"giant aisles, / Rich in model and design" (ll.12–13), the ode is a *tour de
force* whose "rhythm and composition" are nevertheless "hampered," as
Tennyson concedes, by the constraints of its oral performance.

Unlike Tennyson's lyrics and monologues, the ode set to choral recitation has little opportunity to explore the drama of a self-divided mind. It
cannot create a polyphony of voices that allow a monologue or lyric to
mean one thing to the ear in an oral recitation and something else to the
eye in the privacy of a silent reading. Such dramas for the eye and ear are
most finely tuned in poems like "Demeter and Persephone" and "The
Lotos-Eaters," which create slight disparities between the figures of
rhetoric or rhyme that we see on the printed page (*opsis*) and the rhythms
that we hear in the speaking voice solicited from the page (*melos*). The
purpose of such disparities is to raise from the grave of a dead descriptive
language the ghosts of the two-way meanings and multiple ironies that
characterize Tennyson's split personae and their self-divided minds.

Chapter Fourteen

Strong Speech Meets Strong Silence: The Uses of Reserve

Though portions of Tennyson's "Ulysses" can be treated as an actor's script, I want to argue that there are important differences between a speech in a stage play and a dramatic monologue. Even in supplicating a voice from the printed page, Tennyson's best dramatic monologues are often unvoiceable. Whereas a soliloquy from *Hamlet* is meant to be spoken aloud, not even the most experienced actor can hope to reproduce the complex tones conveyed in a silent reading of "Ulysses," "My Last Duchess," or "Andrea del Sarto."

According to Eric Griffiths, a defining feature of dramatic monologues is what Browning in *The Ring and the Book* calls "the printed voice." "The absence of clearly indicated sound from the silence of the written word creates," he says, "a double nature in printed poetry, making it both itself and something other."[1] Included in the half of this "double nature" that aligns a monologue like "Ulysses" with an actor's script are its many "hints at voicing." Using the text as script, a reader who is as skilled an actor as Ulysses will pick up several tricks of voice. He will register the way Tennyson's mariner keeps flouting expectations about casual conversational procedures by repeatedly deploying studied antitheses—"To rust unburnished, not to shine in use," "Though much is taken, much abides" (ll.23, 65)—and by sticking on words like "equal" and "drink": "Unequal laws," "One equal temper"; "I will drink / Life to the lees," "And drunk delight of battle" (ll.4, 68, 6–7, 16). Speaking a fraction too expansively about the dizzying prospect of what he can glimpse through the "arch" of experience or about the vertigo induced by following "knowledge like a sinking star" (l.31), Ulysses veers at other moments to the opposite extreme, contracting language almost to the vanishing point.

As strong speech imposes strong silence on Ulysses' son and fellow mariners, meaning hinges on zero values of tautology and elision: "Death closes all," "He works his work," "that which we are, we are" (ll.51, 43, 67). A good reader will learn to alternate between a leisurely

appositional style and an edgy staccato one, whose sudden choppiness, as
of waves setting in, starts to agitate the speaker: "Come, my friends, /
'Tis not too late to seek a newer world. / Push off. . ." (ll.56–58). Like a
skilled actor, such a reader will be expected to master as subtle yet inef-
faceable tricks of voice Ulysses' habit of saying at once too little and too
much.

Unlike the actors in a stage play, however, readers of "Ulysses" often
feel the impossibility of adjusting their voice to the rapid changes in tone
and to the difficulty of representing in any single reading the several
intonations they imagine as equally appropriate and necessary. Most simply, when we "talk upon paper,"[2] as Barrett Browning says, our words
can be given different patterns of stress, which we may want to linger
over and ponder before making a choice or implicit interpretation, as an
actor would make choices with a script.

One of the pleasures of reading "Ulysses" is the opportunity it affords
for the simultaneity of different imagined (as opposed to actually heard
or spoken) intonations. What contours of voice are we to elicit from the
words, "He works his work, I mine" (l.43)? If we disturb the natural
iambic stress by giving weight to the pronominal adjective "his," the
speaker's tongue may start to curl: we may detect a sneer or slight hint
of contempt in his voice. But if we trust the meter and leave the adjective unstressed, we may prefer, like Dwight Culler,[3] to take the praise of
the "blameless" son (l. 39) at face value, without any trace of irony.

Invoking the mariners as "Souls that have toiled, and wrought, and
thought with [him]" (l.46), Ulysses allows the stressed internal rhymes
to affirm a parity of goals.

> My mariners,
> Souls that have toiled, and wrought, and thought with me—
> That ever with a frolic welcome took
> The thunder and the sunshine, and opposed
> Free hearts, free foreheads—you and I are old;
>
> ("Ulysses," ll.45–49)

Are the words, "you and I are old" (l.49), spoken in a spirit of exhaustion? Are they dragged from Ulysses grudgingly, as a bitter but delayed
concession? Or is their tone, by contrast, celebratory, even buoyant?
Perhaps Ulysses pauses before the dash only to gather up his strength for
a bracing affirmation. Though a silent reading affords the satisfaction of

pondering both possibilities at once, an actor speaking the lines has to opt for one intonation or the other. If the tone is invigorating, even jaunty, then it will be difficult for a speaker to pause tremulously before the dash. How can a bracing recitation hope to intimate that a natural reticence or incomprehension has brought Ulysses to the edge of silence, and that he has crossed the second of his sentence's two framing dashes only reluctantly or in disbelief? Perhaps he cannot truly grasp that he is old.

Often Ulysses' meaning hovers between opposites. If he follows knowledge "like a *sink*ing star," the emphasis falls on the trajectory of his descent. But if the stress shifts to "star," Ulysses is able to move ahead in a final push past the *mysterium tremendum,* "Beyond the utmost bound of human thought" (ll.31–32). Again, is he "*strong* in will" or strong in *will*"? Does his striving make him "strong," or, in his weakened physical state, is he strong only in his resolve to be strong? Should an actor giving a recitation allow the natural iambic stresses to control his intonation of lines 6 and 7: "I cánnot rést from trável; Í will drínk / Life to the leés"? Or in order to make Ulysses' auxiliary verb of volition boldly performative, a form of "doing-by-saying," should the actor force a slight spondaic wrenching of the meter by allowing a light pause or stress on "will" to echo the last phrase in "The Lotos-Eaters": "we wíll not wánder móre"?

In each case, the two alternatives must be imagined rather than heard, since no actor can voice the similes, "like a sinking *star*" and "like a *sink*ing star," simultaneously. Nor can he simultaneously say "strong in *will*" and "*strong* in will." Even in an elegiac monologue by Hardy, "Without Ceremony," only a silent reading can register the two meanings: "So, now that you disappear / *For ever*—in that swift style" and "So, now that you *disappear* / For ever in that swift *style*" (ll.11–12). The first reading dramatizes the finality of the going; the second, the mere habitual manner.

How could an actor, in a dramatic reading of "Ulysses," ever hope to vocalize the poem's important shift from unspoken to spoken thoughts? Up to line 45 Ulysses has been performing in a private theater of the mind. Instead of speaking aloud, he has been musing with himself. Though far more integral to the rest of the poem, this interior monologue has the same explanatory function as the narrative proems to "Oenone," "The Lotos-Eaters," and "Lucretius." If we try to imagine Ulysses communing with himself in a soliloquy, how are the mariners to grasp the difference between words they are meant to hear in the poem's last twenty-five lines and words they are meant to overhear rather than hear before Ulysses turns to address them?

It is difficult in a soliloquy in a play to distinguish between words that are merely thought or imagined and words that are meant to be heard by other actors on the stage. By contrast, a monologue we are invited to read in silence is particularly adept at evoking Ulysses' unheard words, including addresses to Telemachus and the Ithacans that never take place. Ulysses' unflattering portrait of his "savage" subjects, "That hoard, and sleep, and feed, and know not me" (ll.4–5), is made even harsher by the way the caesural pauses of his printed voice break against their hard edges the even harsher precision of verbs—disdainful in themselves—that have been made even more disdainful by being scornfully withheld from the Ithacans. Never having heard the accusation, they have no chance to refute it.

A Galahad by temperament, Ulysses also has difficulty conceiving the satisfactions of his son Telemachus, a Greek King Arthur, whose vocation is "centred," like the medial caesura of line 39, "in the sphere / Of common duties" (ll.39–40). So shadowily conceived is this counterdrama that Ulysses' tribute to Telemachus remains part of a non-tribute, a ceremonial bequeathing of "the scepter and the isle" (l.34) that Ulysses performs only on the stage of his mind, in a conveniently abbreviated rehearsal of the civic ritual. In disclosing such forms of non-presence and non-performance, "Ulysses," a poem supposedly spoken but actually written, reveals an important law of its own genre.

A monologue also provides more opportunity than an actor's script for a poet to speak with two minds upon a subject. To the eye, a simile can attach itself grammatically to more than one noun or verb in its vicinity.

> And this gray spirit yearning in desire
> To follow knowledge like a sinking star
> Beyond the utmost bound of human thought.
>
> (ll.30–32)

A silent reading allows the plummeting star to fall two ways at once. If the simile hooks on to the infinitive phrase, "To follow," it can be construed as a self-deprecating demurrer, a paralipsis, a denial of the sinking spirit's successful pursuit of knowledge in the very act of pursuing it. But if the simile describes not the overreacher's *manner* of pursuit but its *object* (a star "sinking . . . / Beyond the . . . bound), then the vertigo is a product, not of arrogance, but of an epistemological paradox that Tennyson formulates in "The Two Voices" without any hint of criticism.

> 'The highest-mounted mind,' he said,
> 'Still sees the sacred morning spread
> The silent summit overhead.
> ("The Two Voices," ll.79–81)

An actor who is merely using the monologue as a script would have difficulty registering both meanings simultaneously. To pause more over the medial caesura after "knowledge" would emphasize the irony of the spirit's Icarus-like descent. And to minimize the break by voicing the last seven syllables of line 31 in a single span of breath would emphasize (at the expense of the more personal local irony) the general paradox of the infinity of knowledge: Pope's paradox of hills peeping over hills and of Alps on Alps arising. Only in the privacy of a silent reading does it seem possible to register simultaneously the sublime elusiveness of the goal and the ironic retreat of the goal the more closely Ulysses approaches it.

As words break against the line endings, a silent reading of the monologue also allows us to anticipate outcomes that an actor would have difficulty reproducing in an oral recitation. The slight pauses at the ends of lines 6 and 7, for example, invite us to imagine a syntactical completion for the verbs "I will drink" and "I have enjoyed." As we round the corner of line 6, we may be surprised to discover that the speaker's "hungry heart" is voracious, not for food or drink, but for something more elusive, life itself.

> I cannot rest from travel: I will drink
> Life to the lees: all times I have enjoyed
> Greatly, have suffered greatly . . .
> (ll.6–7)

Pausing at the brink of the next line ending, trying to guess what Ulysses will enjoy (battles, travel, "cities of men / And manners"?), we are slightly shocked to discover that, unlike its transitive companion verb, "drink," the verb "enjoy" is too capacious a word to limit itself to a single grammatical object. At the head of the next line Ulysses does indeed qualify his unexpected intransitive use of "enjoyed," but only with a modifier that refuses to limit anything, the adverb "Greatly."

A silent reading of the printed page also reveals how Ulysses fashions words of power, providing a measure of enactment or "doing-by-saying." By pausing after the sixth-syllable caesura in line 22, for example, a skillful actor will show that when Ulysses speaks of pausing, the voice pauses with him.

> How dull it is to pause, to make an end,
> To rust unburnished, not to shine in use!
>
> (ll.22–23)

An actor, however, will be denied the reader's additional pleasure of seeing how the phrase "making an end" coincides with a line ending on the printed page. As the infinitive phrases, "to pause," "to make," "to rust," "to shine," march defiantly ahead, crossing the break at the end of line 22, such a reader will also appreciate the irony of "an end" that marks the midpoint in a chain of phrases that refuse to end.

Unless an actor chooses to voice the second syllable in "aged," which is Christopher Ricks's preferred reading, the sudden contraction of the blank verse to nine syllables in line 3 allows us to *hear* as well as *see* how Ulysses' failure to "mete" or measure out equitable laws extends to a flagging of his poetic "measure" as well.

> Matched with an aged wife, I mete and dole
> Unequal laws unto a savage race, . . .
>
> (ll.3–4)

We can also hear how the long vowels and assonance create an impression of spaciousness so vast that Matthew Arnold felt "these three lines by themselves take up nearly as much time as a whole book of the *Iliad*" (1960, I, p. 147).[4]

> Yet all experience is an arch wherethrough
> Gleams that untravelled world, whose margin fades
> For ever and for ever when I move.
>
> (ll.19–21)

Other subtleties, however, are reserved for silent readings alone. As expansive open vowels with long quantities begin to stretch across the long central line in imitation of the "untravelled world" that gleams alluringly before Ulysses, only a silent reader can see how the "fading margin" of that world also coincides with a slight fading of the poem's right-hand margin on the printed page.

Though a skillful actor can intimate a dimension of enactment, or of "doing-by-saying," in the placement of the second use of "much" before the verb "abides," the effect is easier to register in a silent reading than in an oral recitation.

> Though much is taken, much abides; and though
> We are not now that strength which in old days
> Moved earth and heaven, that which we are, we are—
> (ll.65–67)

Like the repetition of the copulas, the "much" that literally abides in successive feet of the first quoted line enforces what is said. A glance at the printed page also indicates that by the time Ulysses says "Little remains" of his life, only four syllables remain of the two-line clause in which the claim is made.

> Life piled on life
> Were all too little, and of one to me
> Little remains;
> (ll.24–26)

Once again, however, the early-breaking caesura and the prominence given the phrase "Little remains" at the head of a new line are dimensions of enactment that appeal to the eye rather than the ear.

Double grammatical congruities are also easier to pick up in a silent reading of the monologue than in an oral recitation.

> Much have I seen and known; cities of men
> And manners, climates, councils, governments,
> Myself not least, but honoured of them all;
> (ll.13–15)

When read aloud, line 15 tends to rearrange itself as a nominative absolute construction, grammatically detached from the name lists that precede it: Ulysses dramatizes his own self-isolating fame by sundering the syntactical connection between himself and the world. But because we can glance back two lines on the printed page with more ease than we can recall a phrase heard six seconds ago in an oral recitation, it is also more apparent in a silent reading that the pronoun "Myself" most logically functions as the direct object of the principal verbs "seen" and "known." Instead of merely boasting of his honors, despite the modest disclaimer of his phrase "not least," Ulysses is also demonstrating what it means to "become a name" (l.11). In "seeing" and "knowing" *himself,* the real-life Ulysses also has the odd sensation of confronting the legendary Ulysses, an epic version of himself, someone who has just stepped out of Homer's pages. In a silent reading of a monologue a phrase like "Myself not least" often looks two ways at once, creating a chance for a polyphony that no speaking voice can match.

Though Ulysses is identified in a reader's imagination with repeated tricks of voice, often the most meaningful of these repetitions, echoing each other across long spans of verse, will register only on readers who can read the text in silence, attuned to features of syntax and rhythm that they might pass over in an oral recitation. Like the muted allusions to *Hamlet* and *Othello,* the less obvious these repetitions are, the more ironic the disparities they can then create between what the *speaker* hears and what the *poet* and the *reader* hear.

> I mete and dole
> Unequal laws unto a savage race,
> That hoard, and sleep, and feed, and know not me.
>
> (ll.3–5)

> One equal temper of heroic hearts,
> Made weak by time and fate, but strong in will
> To strive, to seek, to find, and not to yield.
>
> (ll.68–70)

The paratactic syntax of line 5 and the triad of infinitive phrases in line 70, each capped by a negative construction, allow two allusive gestures to call to each other across sixty-five intervening lines of verse. Though audible only to attentive readers, who are invited to share private meanings with the ironist behind the speaker's back, the echoes of Hamlet that resound subliminally ("What is a man, / If his chief good and market of his time / Be but to sleep and feed?" IV.iv.33–35) alert us to the presence of other allusions to Shakespeare, unheard by the speaker but picked up by Tennyson and his readers to create ironies at Ulysses' expense.

In denouncing the sluggish behavior of people who "sleep and feed," Hamlet is berating himself for failing to follow the example of the brave but foolhardy Norwegian king, Fortinbras, who is quite prepared to risk the lives of twenty thousand men for a patch of ground too small "To hide the slain" (IV.iv.65). Moreover, when Ulysses, having just berated the Ithacans in words that Hamlet uses to denounce his own "dull revenge," resolves to "shine in use" instead of "rust unburnished" (l.23), he is alluding to a piece of noble-sounding, high-pitched casuistry that Hamlet uses a moment later when trying to glorify Fortinbras' ill-conceived suicide mission against the Poles.

> Sure he that made us with such large discourse,
> Looking before and after, gave us not
> That capability and godlike reason
> To fust in us unused.
>
> (*Hamlet*, IV.iv.36–39)

To recover the context of Ulysses' allusions in Shakespeare is to erode the heroic rhetoric by dissolving it in understated ironies. It is to see how Ulysses' exhortation to his mariners to follow him on a last voyage into death, like Hamlet's defense of risking death "Even for an eggshell" (IV.iv.53), is an excuse for self-destruction.

Having savored the ironies, however, a critic must immediately add that Shakespearean allusions also reveal a secret spring of one of the monologue's chief glories: Ulysses' power to turn his suicide mission into a heroic enterprise. The indictment of rusting "unburnished" instead of shining "in use" reverses Othello's injunction: "Keep up your bright swords, for the dew will rust them" (*Othello* I.ii, 59). Othello's word "dew," like Ulysses' figurative "shine in use," deftly closes off the possibility that any weapons will be literally dewed with blood. And yet the resilient quality of a well-tempered blade is not evoked only to be fenced off or rescinded. It returns at the end of the monologue in the shining metaphor of the mariners' "One equal temper of heroic hearts" (l.68), where their whole physical endowment of heart, lungs, and muscle, keen as a well-tempered sword, is made to strain in unison to the "delight of battle, / Far on the ringing plains of windy Troy" (ll.16–17).

It would be foolish to propose a theory of the monologue on the basis of a single poem, even a representative and justly famous one. As long as we remember, however, that "Ulysses" is less complex than many of Browning's or T. S. Eliot's monologues, it seems possible to say that, unlike soliloquies or other speeches in a stage play like *Becket*, Tennyson's dramatic monologues are not to be treated as actors' scripts or as poems intended for public recitation. The hazards of trying to voice all the subtleties and two-way meanings of a monologue's printed words allow Tennyson to dramatize and explore the precarious status of oral habits in an age of print. In a dramatic monologue, as in a closet drama like Browning's *Paracelsus,* the script (or text of the character's speech) is meant to be read silently. The real action takes place in the private theater of our minds.

But an important difference remains between the two genres. Because each speech in a closet drama is treated as a set piece in relative isolation from all the other speeches, sustained impersonation of the speakers is seldom really possible. The structural component in *Paracelsus* is not (as in a stage play) the relation of speech to speech, or (as in a dramatic monologue) the interplay of speaker, silent auditor, and dramatic occasion. Browning builds his closet drama out of declamations or orations, the equivalent of the tirades in "Locksley Hall," which often resemble arias in an opera. Accordingly, while the silent performance of a dramatic monologue points the genre in the direction of a closet drama, its genius for impersonation preserves an even stronger link between an actor's public performance in a stage play and the reader's private staging of a monologue. As one commentator says, dramatic monologues "are profoundly untheatrical just because they make the reader himself a theatre, and so dispense with the externalized elements of theatrical performance."[5] Since the monologue's subtlest dramatic effects are often unvoiceable by any physical voice we could hear on a stage, Ulysses' strong speech should ideally confront the equally strong silence of the reader, who is meant to impersonate the speaker by aspiring in a private theater of the mind to the active silence of Ulysses' responsive but vigilant mariners.

A monologue like "Ulysses" creates one drama for the ear and another for the eye. The conversational voice that readers solicit from the printed page seems to be spontaneous and free, independent of the poet's control. This autonomous voice has an unusual feature, however: it offers a spoken drama for the ear that turns out to be slightly at odds with the monologue's silent visual drama of half revealing and half concealing highly wrought rhetorical patterns and grammatical forms of approximately the same size and shape. Artfully fabricated by the poet behind the mask, these forms are a feature of *opsis* rather than *melos*. I am thinking, for example, of the double placement of the word "end" at the end of a poetic line ("something ere the end"; "How dull it is to pause, to make an end"—ll.51, 22), and of the recurrent use of verbal triads followed by a negative infinitive: "That hoard, and sleep, and feed, and know not me"; "To strive, to seek, to find, and not to yield" (ll.5, 70). Indeed the more carefully we study the monologue's optical patterns, its drama for the eye, the more we realize that its drama for the ear is not as spontaneous or free of Tennyson's constructive control as we might think. Rather, the lyrical and grammatical forms that are easiest to enjoy in a silent reading of the monologue exhibit what Ralph Rader calls a "completely artificial presentation of what seems" at first a "completely independent natural activity."[6]

But instead of limiting dramatic monologues proper to poems whose spontaneous speech patterns create a spoken drama for the ear (as Ralph Rader proposes), I prefer to take as a defining feature of the genre the odd assortments of spoken words and lyric shapes—the slight disparities between *melos* and *opsis*, which are accessible only in a silent reading of a Tennyson monologue. Though "Ulysses" is a poem of one-sided conversation, the little conflicts it stages between *melos* and *opsis* are marks of a self-divided mind. They express the pull and counterpull of a split persona who favors the open and the free, and a readiness for something new. The discourse in such a poem is not monological at all, in Mikhail Bakhtin's sense, but "dialogical." It is "an occasion for interaction," as G. S. Morson says, "in which differences" between the speaker and the poet "can produce new and unforeseen possibilities."[7]

Chapter Fifteen
Words of Power: Imitation and Allusion

Tennyson's allusions are never simply slavish imitations of the gestures and accents of magnanimity. Like the imitations of the Renaissance humanists, they are authentic creative acts, examples of what J. L. Austin calls performative utterances. As words of power, these allusions do not passively record a meaning that antecedently exists. Their meaning is a form of "doing-by-saying," created in the act of alluding, and leading ultimately to original expression.

Tennyson's boldest claim for the performative power of poetic language is his early ode, "The Poet." In alluding to Shelley's "Ode to the West Wind," Tennyson transforms Shelley's symbol of "winged seeds" by combining it with the "viewless arrows of [the poet's] thoughts," "headed / And winged with flame" (ll.11–12). Shelley's wind, a Romantic equivalent of the Holy Spirit, is equated in Tennyson's ode with the poet's oracular power to shake "the world" with his "word."

> And when she spake,
>
> Her words did gather thunder as they ran,
>   And as the lightning to the thunder
> Which follows it, riving the spirit of man,
>   Making earth wonder,
>
> So was their meaning to her words. No sword
>   Of wrath her right arm whirled,
> But one poor poet's scroll, and with *his* word
>   She shook the world.
>
>   ("The Poet," ll.48–56)

Extending the voice across successive stanzaic breaks, in graceful arches of gathering sound, the run-ons cover greater intervals of space and time than an ode can normally span. The power of words to create something new, like God's creation by verbal fiat, allows Tennyson to use as well as mention Shelley's doctrine of bloodless revolution through the spread of prophecy and truth.

Sometimes Tennyson's most resonant allusions are allusions to other allusions, like Bedivere's echo of Milton's echo of Virgil. Harking back to the narrator's self-correction in "Oenone"—"and round her neck / Floated her hair or seemed to float in rest" (ll.17–18), Tennyson's claim that Bedivere "saw . . . / Or thought he saw" King Arthur's boat ("The Passing of Arthur," ll.463–65) summons up Aeneas' seeing the dim form of Dido through the shadows of the Virgilian underworld, "as early in the month one sees, or thinks he has seen, the moon rise amid clouds" ("aut videt aut vidisse putat," *Aeneid*, 6.454).

But even as Tennyson recalls the moment in Virgil when Aeneas glimpses his cherished but ill-used Dido, he also evokes and reinvents the most important earlier use of this Virgilian allusion in English poetry. For behind Virgil's simile we hear the diminishing epic simile Milton uses in *Paradise Lost* to reduce the conclave of demons to elves seen at midnight.

> Behold a wonder! they but now who seemd
> In bigness to surpass Earths Giant Sons
> Now less than smallest Dwarfs, in narrow room
> Throng numberless, like that Pigmean Race
> Beyond the *Indian* Mount, or Faerie Elves,
> Whose midnight Revels, by a Forrest side
> Or Fountain some belated Peasant sees,
> Or dreams he sees, . . .
>
> (*Paradise Lost*, I.777–84)

Milton's simile works two ways at once. The diminishing wand that turns earth's "Giant Sons" to dwarves allows Milton to dwell for a moment on the irrelevant marvels of a midsummer night's dream. But the dream's enchantment also exaggerates the bathos and indignity of Satan's defeated forces, shrunk to the size of pygmies trying to squeeze into Pandemonium.

Tennyson does not merely mirror Milton's and Virgil's infernal impressions. Though Arthur's defeat has its infernal moments, Tennyson reinvents his sources by using the diminishing size of Arthur's ship to enlarge rather than diminish his hero's stature. Instead of being glimpsed fitfully through moonlit shadows, like Virgil's Dido or Milton's elves, Arthur is said to "vanish," not into shade, as we expect, but "into light" (l.468). More importantly, the hesitancies of mood and syntax that are so exquisite a quality of Virgil's verse keep diffusing and expanding until they become the most remarkable feature of Tennyson's allusion.

> Thereat once more he moved about, and clomb
> Even to the highest he could climb, and saw,
> Straining his eyes beneath an arch of hand,
> Or thought he saw, the speck that bare the King,
> Down that long water opening on the deep
> Somewhere far off, pass on and on, and go
> From less to less and vanish into light.
> And the new sun rose bringing the new year.
> ("The Passing of Arthur," ll.462–69)

The coda immediately qualifies the certitude of "saw" with Virgil's and Milton's provisional "Or thought he saw" (ll.463, 465); and even the sun that "rose bringing the new year" (l.469) is the neutral sun of the Sermon on the Mount, which God "maketh . . . to arise on the evil and the good" alike (Matthew 5:45). The cautious advance and retreat are gravely barren. Using a *tmesis* to insert a protracted participial phrase—"Straining his eyes beneath an arch of hand" (l.464)—between the verb "saw" and its grammatical complement, Tennyson even seems reluctant to let his allusion to Virgil sound more resonantly than Milton's own prior echo of Virgil.

Like the return to hell of Milton's narrator, however, after his momentary seduction by the enchantments of elfland, Tennyson's motions backward to the real and the observed give an impression of tremendous honesty. The insistent couplings of "clomb" and "climb," "saw" and "saw," the passing "on and on," then going from "less to less" before dissolving, show Bedivere, not spellbound like Aeneas or enchanted like Milton's peasant, but intently scrutinizing, as he looks harder and harder at the shrinking object. Even when the concluding lines are not strictly enjambed, the syntax propels us forward, without full pauses, so that there is no rest until the last two lines: "From less to less and vanish into light. / And the new sun rose bringing the new year" (ll.468–69). The penultimate line affirms the completion of a pattern; and, like the alexandrine at the end of a Spenserian stanza, the last line signals closure by stepping up the number of accents from five to six. But countering the terminal features of night, autumn, passing on and on, and vanishing are two events not found in Tennyson's sources: the rising of the sun and the advent of another year. The closing words are not—significantly—words of decline into a Virgilian or Miltonic underworld, but words that break out of closure.

Like Shakespeare in *King Lear,* Tennyson is more preoccupied than most poets with the enigma of premature endings and with the stubborn unfolding of dramas beyond their expected termination points. Speakers like St. Simeon and Tithonus want their poems to end. Death is their only escape from monologues that have been ready to end almost from the moment they begin. In other poems like *In Memoriam* the ending comes too soon. Hallam's premature death, like the death of Tennyson's son Lionel, refuses to fulfill the generic promise inherent in any biography. The drama of Hallam's life is formally concluded with the coming of his burial ship in section 12 of *In Memoriam*. But the substance of that long elegy is still in urgent progress, rolling across and crushing the very framework of closure that helps the reader isolate and limit the confusion or disorder in a short verse epistle like Tennyson's elegy for his son.

> And saying; 'Comes he thus, my friend?
> Is this the end of all my care?'
> And circle moaning in the air:
> 'Is this the end? Is this the end?'
> (*In Memoriam*, XII.13–16)

The mourner alludes to Kent's ineffectual interruption of Lear's agony: "Is this the promised end?" (*King Lear* V.iii.264). In neither *In Memoriam* nor *King Lear,* however, does the promise of an afterlife put a comfortable frame around the life that has just ended. The promise is formulated as a question, and as a question about ends in a quatrain, a canto, and a poem that all refuse to end.

Reading "St. Simeon Stylites" is like reading a farcical version of *King Lear.* We are waiting for a death that has been prepared "For ages and for ages" (l.98) and that now seems overdue. But the more Simeon anticipates his end the more it eludes him. For the aspiring martyr his

monologue is too long, almost unendurably so. Near the beginning
Simeon prophesies:

> my end draws nigh;
> I hope my end draws nigh:
> ("St. Simeon Stylites," ll.35–36)

But each time he repeats the word "end" it moves farther away from a
line ending on the printed page. Simeon stretches us out upon the rack
of his suffering by trying to end an action that, despite all efforts to ter-
minate it at "A quarter before twelve" (l.218), is still in urgent progress
when the monologue concludes.

> The end! the end!
> Surely the end! What's here? a shape, a shade,
> A flash of light. Is that the angel there
> That holds a crown?
> ("St. Simeon Stylites," ll.198–201)

Like Kent's disturbing query about promised ends and endings in *King
Lear,* the problem of knowing when something ends is also, in one
critic's words, "a variation on the problems of knowing *if* something
ends and whether it will ever end."[1]

Tennyson's allusions to *Antony and Cleopatra* in his play *Queen Mary* are
less subtle, more elaborately parodic. Cardinal Pole, who under different
circumstances might have been Mary's lover and consort, describes his
return to England on the River Thames in an unintentionally mock-epic
allusion to Cleopatra's first appearance to her lover Antony on the river
Cydnus (II.ii.195–223). In Shakespeare's blank verse the lovesick winds
and amorous water combine with the leisurely run-ons to celebrate an
opulent fusion of the five senses and four elements. The visual appeal of
the beaten gold, purple sails, and silver oars commingle with the smell of
strange perfume, the touch of flower-soft hands and glowing cheeks, and
even the sound of flute music. A moment later Antony is invited to a
supper which he is too lovesick to eat: he feasts with his eyes only. Like
the five senses, each of the four elements plays its appointed role: the
water is amorous of the boat, which burns on the water. Only Antony is
left stranded on land, as even the air seems on the point of vacating the

marketplace to gaze on Cleopatra. There is no vacancy of either sense or element in this brimming scene.

By comparison, the lean conjurings of Cardinal Pole are pinched and meager (*Queen Mary*, III.ii, vol. 8, pp. 89–90). Pole adds amorous touches, trying to make Philip a Spanish Antony and Mary an English Cleopatra. He even adds a strain of religious allusion that turns the cedar throne into the exotic cedar of Lebanon tree that Maud's lover consecrates: "Lo, now you are enclosed with boards of cedar, / Our little sister of the Song of Songs!" But the cedar boards are too suggestive of a throne turned into a coffin to rival the ostentation of Antony's and Cleopatra's love in Shakespeare or even the lover's exotic apostrophe to the cedar of Lebanon tree in *Maud*.

Instead of enthroning Cleopatra or even Philip on the royal barge, the conceited Pole enthrones himself. The strain of egotism is never absent. It is as if Shakespeare's Cleopatra were to praise herself, instead of allowing Enorbarus to do it for her. Even "that long low minster," the dismal church where Mary and Philip were married, is depressed in memory and affection by the dragging spondees and harsh successive stresses of Pole's description, which lengthens out its gloom.

In *Queen Mary* the exotic play of Shakespeare's colors has been filtered through a sieve of chaste silver-white impressions. The waves are no longer amorous of the barge, but twinkle in a diamond dance that mirrors the sparkling of the silver cross before the prow. Though the allusions to Cleopatra are a *tour de force* designed to estrange the familiar and domesticate the strange, the only apparent miracle has a wholly natural explanation. The river that flows away from the sea, in apparent defiance of natural law, is simply rising with the tide. Though the sun burns the Thames, as Cleopatra's burnished throne burns the water, Tennyson evokes a distinctly northern setting, where ever-encroaching fog blankets the green under a snow-like pall.

The most pervasive allusions and the single most authentic imitation in Tennyson's canon are not Shakespearean, however, but Spenserian. His poetry abounds in Spenserian echoes, and in one Spenserian imitation, "The Lotos-Eaters," Tennyson carries Spenserianism far beyond Keats's achievement in "The Eve of St. Agnes."

An important feature of Spenser's style that Tennyson shares with Keats is the ability to capture visual effects through sound. Northrop Frye asserts that the most sustained mastery of such effects in English occurs in *The Faerie Queene*.[2] Like Spenser's line, "The Eugh obedient to the bender's will" (*Faerie Queene*, I.i.9), where the weak syllables in the middle "sag out in a bow shape," Tennyson's alexandrine in "The Lotos-Eaters"—"The mild-eyed melancholy Lotos-eaters came" (l.27)—uses a long Latin word to lighten the rhythm. The weak syllables droop at the center, in imitation of the mariners' drooping spirits. This line also illustrates another feature of Spenser's style: the use of polysyllabic words to span feet and to counterpoint in their individual rhythms the line's dominant meter. In line 27, "The mild-eyed melancholy Lotos-eaters came," the rising iambic motion of Tennyson's alexandrine is offset by the falling trochaic character of each of the adjectives, which create a dying fall characteristic of Spenser and (as Alan Sinfield has shown) *In Memoriam*.

Spenser's influence is most apparent in the Spenserian stanzas of Tennyson's proem to "The Lotos-Eaters." But even in the choric song, which adapts Spenser's description of the "trickling streame" and "ever-drizzling raine" (*Faerie Queene* I.i.41) that lull Morpheus to sleep, Tennyson writes in an appositional Spenserian style that defers the principal verbs and makes skillful use of indefinite caesuras. The mariners' searching indictment of creation, "Why should we only toil, the roof and crown of things?" (l.69), echoes Phaedria's appeal to Cymochles (*Faerie Queene* II.vi.17). In the fourth strophe the easeful allure of death, which the mariners welcome as "the end of life" (l.86), repeats the casuistry of Spenser's Despair: "Death is the end of woes" (*Faerie Queene* I.ix.47). Finally, in the mariners' culminating resolve to seek rest after "labour in the deep mid-ocean" (l.172), we hear an equally enticing echo of the mermaids' appeal to Guyon and the palmer as they travel to the Bower of Bliss: "This is the Port of rest from troublous toyle" (*Faerie Queene* II.xii.32).

Spenser's influence is equally evident in "The Lady of Shalott," where Tennyson alludes to the magic mirror in which Britomart sees reflected the image of Artegall (*Faerie Queene* III.ii.20, 24). Tennyson gives greater prominence to the Spenserian elements by moving to the head of the sixth stanza the mirror in which the Lady sees reflected the knight's reflection in another mirror—the river.

In the Spenserian alexandrine of the last refrain of Tennyson's song "The Splendour Falls on Castle Walls" we can hear in the echoed word "answer" a fading echo of Spenser's *Epithalamion* refrain. If the stars are merry in *Maud*, it is partly because they imitate another line in Spenser's sumptuous marriage poem: "All night therefore attend your merry play" (*Epithalamion* l.368). But the more Tennyson assimilates into *Maud*'s garden poetry the festive celebrations in Spenser's *Epithalamion*, the more diffused his Spenserianism becomes. We might risk a paradox and say that it is precisely because Tennyson's vision in *Maud* is so authentically Spenserian that it ceases to be consciously modeled on Spenser. As Tennyson, like Spenser, achieves the symbolic range of a miniature biblical epic in which Maud is both Eve and Mary, the virgin of the *hortus conclusus* of the Song of Songs, we sense that these garden lyrics are less a Spenserian imitation than the kind of vision that all pastoral poetry— from the Bible to Spenser—exists to express.

Tennyson's explanation that Arthur is "Ideal manhood closed in real man" ("To the Queen," l.38) owes more to Tasso's outline of the allegory in *Gerusalemme liberata* than to Spenser's elaboration of his allegory in the letter to Raleigh. Yet in embracing the drift of epic toward psychology and romance, Tennyson is continuing Spenser's own practice. Gareth's most formidable opponent, the Star of Evening, though curiously resilient like Spenser's Maleger, is physically decrepit. In Gareth's last antagonist, Tennyson parodies Spenser's sad and serious portrait of Night, the progenitor of Duessa, the mere counterfeit of light (*Faerie Queene* I.v.20–45). Even the collapse of Tennyson's pasteboard figure, who as a "blooming boy" proves the least dangerous of Gareth's opponents, makes mock-heroic use of Artegall's misdirected attack on the armed Britomart (*Faerie Queene* IV.vi.19). Few passages in Tennyson better illustrate the growing separation of sign and referent in Victorian allegory.

As Tennyson more directly identifies each successive adversary with a psychological reaction in the mind of Gareth and the reader, these parodic Malegers and Britomarts, like other characters in *Idylls of the King*, become familiar and untamed potentialities of every heart and mind. Readers who seek the comfort of allegorical understanding are made to feel as insecure as Arthur. They lack the assurance of any vantage point from which to hammer into certainty Arthur's platitudes about prayer or Merlin's weird prophecies about dying to come again. It is as if Tennyson were continually using allegory to subvert allegory. If he finds he can be most contemporary by being most medieval, most psychological and agnostic by being most Spenserian, it is because few poets have a deeper grasp of Spenser's own deep feeling for the emblems of inwardness and mystery.

When Bulwer-Lytton accused Tennyson of "out-babying Wordsworth" and "out-glittering Keats," his barb drew attention to important similarities among the three poets. Tennyson's "Tithonus" is saturated with allusions to Keats's odes: even his use of the detachable and slow-moving blank-verse line, which lacks the forward thrust of

Milton's blank verse, is Keatsian. Yet to paraphrase Virgil, it is harder to
steal a line from Keats than to steal the club of Hercules. Whereas the
notion of becoming a sod to the nightingale's "high requiem" swells into
a strong revulsion against death in "Ode to a Nightingale," Tithonus
welcomes a one-way trip from dust to dust, ashes to ashes. Unlike Keats,
who says farewell to the bird with a heavy heart, Tithonus masters the
horror of leave-taking by defining, with restraint, a farewell that is forever—a farewell that will not, and need not, be spoken again. As in the
ode "To Autumn," loss tells chiefly as a consecration of remembering and
an enriched autumnal tone.

In both "Tithonus" and "Ode to a Nightingale" the "deceiving fancy"
first contrives a union of sensuous immediacy and permanence, and in
each case the quest for union fails. Though warm and passionate, like
most things temporal, Aurora's heart is always "renewed" and her
"bosom" always beating, for like the lovers on Keats's Grecian urn she is
"All breathing human passion far above." But as oblivion crystallizes
with terrifying literalness into Tithonus' image of himself, "earth in
earth," the search for permanence starts to break down. There follows a
touching change of focus, comparable to Keats's sudden thought of no
longer hearing the nightingale or of contemplating in place of ravishing
passion a mere cold pastoral on the urn. Since a lyric apostrophe to the
dawn may strike Tennyson as archaic or strained, he wholly naturalizes
the convention by substituting for the Romantic lyric's apostrophe to a
bird the dramatic monologue's convention of a one-sided conversation
with a silent auditor.

Just as the nightingale soars into a timeless world that Keats cannot
enter, so Tithonus uses words of power to detach the linear journey of his
own return to earth from the circular trip of the goddess. "Thou wilt
renew thy beauty morn by morn" (l.74) is both a prophecy and a decree.
It sounds like the final compromise Tennyson is offering for a dozen
more elaborate endings. To evoke the end is to accept the end, to surrender the personality to the apostrophized auditor for whom there is no
end. The objectivity of the closure is therefore moral. As in Keats's odes,
it obliterates the mind's pathetic fallacies, in a conquest of sentimental
attachment to the object defined.

At the climax of *In Memoriam* Tennyson alludes to an older Romantic
poet. He puts his elegy under pressure by turning Wordsworth's experience of a diffused "presence" in "Tintern Abbey" into a ritual decree. In a
kind of baptism, in which Hallam receives a felicitous new epithet,
Tennyson assimilates the dead man's voice to the rolling air.

> Thy voice is on the rolling air;
>> I hear thee where the waters run;
>> Thou standest in the rising sun,
> And in the setting thou art fair.

> What art thou then? I cannot guess;
>> But though I seem in star and flower
>> To feel thee some diffusive power,
> I do not therefore love thee less:
>>>> (*In Memoriam*, 130.1–8)

In summoning up an echo of Wordsworth's

>> sense sublime
> Of something far more deeply interfused,
> Whose dwelling is the light of setting suns,
> And the round ocean and the living air,
> And the blue sky, and in the mind of man:
>>> ("Tintern Abbey," ll.95–99),

Tennyson expects us to remember how Wordsworth's strident anaphora and expansive meter, pressing ahead in keeping with the paratactic syntax that assimilates spirit to nature, eliminate the possibility of an important elegiac convention. Confident that "Eternal form shall still divide / The eternal soul from all beside" (*In Memoriam* 47.6–7), Tennyson had hoped to talk with the dead Hallam as familiarly as Milton's swain addresses Lycidas. Instead, in the running waters and the rolling air, in the rising and the setting sun, he encounters something more Wordsworthian and less Miltonic, a presence at once more sublime and less personal, than he anticipated.

Tennyson's mourner finally faces up to the painful truth that some great goods cannot exist together. Any choice between the intimate and the sublime, the personal and the cosmic, is likely to entail some irreparable loss. Though experiencing such losses is one of the things that make us human, Tennyson cannot bear to admit that values like intimacy and sublimity may actually exist in inverse proportion and so be incapable of being reconciled in some greater whole. The very presence in the elegy of a diffusive voice hints at what is missing and how the genre itself has been disturbed and transformed.

Epilogue

As scholarly and critical studies too often show, it is easier to bury Tennyson than to praise him. A proper estimate of his achievement must demonstrate how he brought to his poems of politics and state a poise of values and a balance of mind finer than anything since Marvell's *Ode* on Cromwell. It must also include an awareness of the large historic vision in *Idylls of the King,* which maintains a direct and living contact with the medieval romances of Malory and the Renaissance heroic poems of Spenser and Milton. Exploring the conflicts of a self-divided mind in "Ulysses" and "Tithonus," Tennyson also reinvents the most resourceful and characteristic of nineteenth-century poetic forms: the dramatic monologue.

In *In Memoriam* Tennyson writes a poem more personal than any he had written, but one that also engages the most inclusive philosophic and scientific interests of his contemporaries. Combining the short Romantic lyric of loss with conventions of the Augustinian confession, Tennyson's mourner turns his refinement of a spare and broken-hearted voice, attenuated by frugal tetrameter quatrains, into the more copious music of a Victorian *Essay on Man.* Few elegies can combine a grievous reticence at their core with such huge trajectories of meditation, thrown like an arch over long intervals of time.

A virtuoso by twentieth-century standards, Tennyson is as much at home in Taoist and Buddhist speculation as he is in the geological thought of Robert Chambers and Charles Lyell. He brings to his study of the post-Kantian idealists, including *The Institutes of Metaphysics* of his friend, the Scottish philosopher J. F. Ferrier, the same informed interest and understanding that he brings to his study of both Lamarckian and nonteleological theories of biological evolution.

Though an heir to the Romantic poets, enjoying an easy commerce with Wordsworth and Keats, Tennyson is also a Roman poet, who deeply assimilates Virgil, Lucretius, and especially the conversational social idiom of Horace, whom he despised as a schoolboy. He has an affinity with the propriety of feeling, civilized intimacy, and instinct for social life and manners of Horace and the English Augustan poets, Dryden and Pope, who turned letter-writing into a minor art. Despite the separation of poetry from society, which he proclaims in "The Poet's Mind" and

"The Palace of Art," Tennyson's profounder sympathies are for the grave courtesies and delicate feelings expressed in verse epistles to such friends as F. D. Maurice, Edward Fitzgerald, and Benjamin Jowett, and in his gracious invitation "To Mary Boyle." From Horace and the Augustan poets Tennyson learns to be intimate and casual without loss of dignity and to make use of other poets' resources while still refining the highly individual and civilized discourse of a small group of friends.

As Poet Laureate, Tennyson also affirms the public role of the artist, the classical (and also Shelleyan) idea that the poet is an energetic civilizer and an unacknowledged legislator of the world. Tennyson's most valuable gift to successors like Arnold and T. S. Eliot is his perfection of a generously allusive poetry that can help readers become less parochial by learning to see life steadily and see it whole. The civilizing force of this ideal, which he had first learned from the epic poetry of Milton and Virgil, can be poignantly felt in Tennyson's tribute to the Roman poet he most admires and resembles:

> Light among the vanished ages; star that gildest yet this phantom
> shore;
> Golden branch amid the shadows, kings and realms that pass to rise
> no more;
>
> ("To Virgil," ll.13–14)

The long rolling measure sustains a breadth of vision and a sureness of rhythm that evoke the poise of the Virgilian hexameter. But the triumphal beginning soon becomes the vision of "Ilion falling, Rome arising" (l.2), which prepares for the decline of all civilizations, and Tennyson's personal, scrutinizing vision of the world itself as a "phantom shore" (l.13).

Just as Aeneas takes a last glimpse of Achilles and Dido in Virgil's underworld, so, as we in this epilogue cast a last look back at Tennyson, one of the saddest and most civilized of Western poets, we can see him, like his beloved Virgil, brooding over "the doubtful doom of human kind" in the gravest line of the poem, and in—significantly—the last stanza to be written.

> Thou that seëst Universal Nature moved by Universal Mind;
> Thou majestic in thy sadness at the doubtful doom of human kind;
>
> ("To Virgil," ll.11–12)

As Tennyson lingers fondly over the achievements of his great precursor, the falling trochees add regret to a backward-reaching intimacy that, like any profound encounter with the past, partly cancels the "doom" by linking the generations. Renewed and refined in these elegiac lines "To Virgil," which Douglas Bush praises as the "the briefest and finest appreciation" of the classical poet "ever written,"[1] Tennyson's achievement as a civilizing poet of allusion can confidently be left to justify itself. Like the pursuit of virtue or a liberal education, the study of such poetry and the tradition it honors is its own reward.

Notes and References

Preface

    1. T. S. Eliot, *"In Memoriam," Selected Essays* (London: Faber and Faber, 1932), 328.

    2. Richard Wollheim, *The Thread of Life* (Cambridge, Mass.: Harvard University Press, 1984), 154–59.

Part I: Genres in the Making

    1. F. E. L. Priestley, *Language and Structure in Tennyson's Poetry* (London: André Deutsch Ltd., 1973), 68.

Chapter One

    1. Mieke Bal, *Narratology: Introduction to the Theory of Narrative* (Toronto: University of Toronto Press, 1985), 146: "When the primary fabula and the embedded fabula can be paraphrased in such a manner that both paraphrases have one or more elements in common, the subtext is a *sign* of the primary text. The place of the embedded text—the mirror-text—in the primary text determines its function for the reader."

    2. Except for the plays, all Tennyson quotations are taken from the three-volume Longmans edition by Christopher Ricks, *The Poems of Tennyson* (London and Harlow: Longmans, Green, 1987). Quotations from *Queen Mary* and *Becket* are from *The Works of Tennyson,* ed. Hallam Lord Tennyson (London: Macmillan, 1908), vols. 8 and 9, respectively. Since Hallam's Eversley edition does not number the lines in the plays, to make the quotations easier to locate I have provided the page number in each volume after the act and scene numbers.

    3. Quoted by Hallam Tennyson in *Alfred Lord Tennyson: A Memoir* (London: Macmillan, 1897), II, 364.

    4. Quoted by A. Dwight Culler in *The Poetry of Tennyson* (New Haven and London: Yale University Press, 1977), 263.

    5. Culler, 117.

    6. Thomas Carlyle, *The Works of Thomas Carlyle* (London: Chapman and Hall, 1898–1901), I, 212.

    7. Gerhard Joseph, *Tennysonian Love: The Strange Diagonal* (Minneapolis: University of Minnesota Press, 1969).

    8. J. F. Ferrier, *The Institutes of Metaphysics: Theory of Knowing and Being* (Edinburgh and London: Blackwood, 1854), 93.

Chapter Two

1.   The phrase is Joseph Allen Boone's, in *Tradition Counter Tradition: Love and the Form of Fiction* (Chicago and London: University of Chicago Press, 1987), 16.

For feminist readings of *The Princess,* often unsympathetic to Tennyson, see Kate Millet, *Sexual Politics* (Garden City, N.Y.: Doubleday, 1970), 76–80; Nina Auerbach, *Communities of Women: An Idea in Fiction* (Cambridge, Mass.: Harvard University Press, 1978), 106–12; Eve Kosofsky Sedgwick, *Between Men: English Literature and Male Homosocial Desire* (New York: Columbia University Press, 1985), 118–35; Marjorie Stone, "Genre Subversion and Gender Inversion: *The Princess* and *Aurora Leigh,*" *Victorian Poetry* 25 (1987), 101–27; and Marion Shaw, *Alfred Lord Tennyson* (Atlantic Highlands, N.J.: Humanities Press International), 115–20.

2.   On comparable challenges to "the self-proclaimed universality of the marriage plot" in Victorian fiction, see Boone's essay "Wedlock as Deadlock and Beyond" in *Tradition Counter Tradition,* 1–27.

Chapter Three

1.   Peter Coveney and Richard Highfield, *The Arrow of Time: A Voyage Through Science to Solve Time's Mystery* (New York: Fawcett Columbine, 1990), 169.

2.   Søren Kierkegaard, *Stages on Life's Way,* trans. David F. Svenson and Walter Lowrie (Princeton: Princeton University Press, 1940), 30.

Chapter Four

1.   Nina Auerbach, *Private Theatricals: The Lives of the Victorians* (Cambridge, Mass.: Harvard University Press, 1990), 95. "Dying as Tennyson's saint, not as a private man, Irving acted out the public, spectacular nature of all imagined death. Not only was dying never obscure, but, with Tennyson as its laureate, it was never real."

2.   Hélène Cixous, *"Coming to Writing" and Other Essays,* ed. Deborah Jenson (Cambridge, Mass.: Harvard University Press, 1991), 4.

3.   Ibid., 3.

4.   Phillipe Ariès, *The Hour of Our Death,* trans. by Helen Weaver (New York: Knopf, 1981), 405–6, 442–46. Ariès calls the nineteenth century the age "of the beautiful death." He associates it with "the temporary survival" of Cathy's cadaver in *Wuthering Heights,* with "the physical beauty" of her death, and with the "vertigo that [her] plunge into death produces in" Heathcliff (p. 405). A wild or "untamed" death," which Ariès also associates with the rise of Romanticism, allows the fear of death, no longer "channeled into familiar rites," to cross "the threshold into the unspeakable, the inexpressible" (405).

5. Tom Stoppard, *Rosencrantz and Guildenstern are Dead* (London: Faber and Faber, 1967), 62.

6. Ibid.

7. Randall Jarrell, *Poetry and the Age* (New York: Knopf, 1953), 68.

8. Stoppard, 61.

9. Quoted by Chaim Potok, *The Chosen* (New York: Fawcett Crest, 1967), 193.

Chapter Five

1. W. B. Yeats, "Edmund Spenser," in *Essays and Introductions* (New York: Collier, 1961), 367.

2. Northrop Frye, *Words With Power* (New York, Harcourt Brace, 1990), 83.

3. Christopher Ricks, "The Antithetical Sense," *Beckett's Dying Words* (Oxford: Oxford University Press, 1993), 128–45.

4. Ibid., 136.

5. For other approaches to *Idylls of the King* readers should consult the following book-length studies: J. M. Gray, *Thro' the Vision of the Night* (Montreal: McGill-Queen's Press, 1980), John R. Reed, *Perception and Design in Tennyson's 'Idylls of the King'* (Athens, Ohio: Ohio University Press, 1969), John D. Rosenberg, *The Fall of Camelot: A Study of Tennyson's 'Idylls of the King'* (Cambridge, Mass.: Harvard University Press, 1973), and Clyde de L. Ryals, *From the Great Deep: Essays on 'Idylls of the King'* (Athens, Ohio: Ohio University Press, 1973).

Part Two: A Ventriloquized World

1. Douglas Bush, "Alfred, Lord Tennyson," in *Major British Writers,* ed. G. B. Harrison (New York: Harcourt, Brace, 1954), 376.

2. W. J. Fox, review of *Tennyson's Poems, Chiefly Lyrical, Westminster Review* 14 (1831), reprinted in *Victorian Scrutinies,* ed. Isobel Armstrong (London: Athlone, 1972), 77.

Chapter Six

1. William Empson, *Using Biography* (Cambridge, Mass.: Harvard University Press, 1984), 132, 142, 144.

2. Philip Sidney, *An Apologie for Poetrie,* ed. J. Churton Collins (Oxford: Clarendon Press, 1950), 44.

In his Oxford *Lectures on Poetry* Keble tries to explain why Lucretius, a poet who "acknowledges neither Author nor Ruler of Nature," should be "lauded as high-priest and interpreter of this very Nature?" His answer is that the Roman atheist unknowingly foreshadows the Christian revelation. See especially *Keble's Lectures on Poetry 1832–1841,* trans. E. K. Francis (Oxford: Clarendon Press, 1912), vol. 2, 333–34, 320.

    3. Christopher Ricks, *Tennyson* (Macmillan: New York, 1972), 275.

    4. Ralph Rader, "The Dramatic Monologue and Related Lyric Forms," *Critical Inquiry* 3 (1976), 135.

Chapter Seven

    1. Richard Wollheim, *The Thread of Life* (Cambridge, Mass.: Harvard University Press, 1984), 154–59.

    2. Ibid., 157.

    3. Ibid., 157–58.

    4. Ibid., 191.

Chapter Eight

    1. Jean-Paul Sartre, "Bad Faith," in *Being and Nothingness,* trans. Hazel E. Barnes (New York: Washington Square Press, 1966), 86–116.

    2. John Keble, *Lectures on Poetry, 1832–1841,* trans. E. K. Francis, vol. 2 (Oxford: Clarendon Press, 1912), 333–34.

    3. Sartre, 94.

    4. Oscar Wilde, *De Profundis* (New York: Vintage, 1964), 125.

    5. Ibid.

    6. Ibid.

Chapter Nine

    1. On "the charismatic power of illness, mental or otherwise, in women" see Nina Auerbach, *Private Theatricals: The Lives of the Victorians* (Cambridge, Mass.: Harvard University Press, 1990), 80. "Women might be barred from heroics, relegated to the privacy of illness and solitary visions, but nineteenth-century theatricality energized these illnesses and visions with transforming glory" (83).

Chapter Ten

    1. A. Dwight Culler, *The Poetry of Tennyson* (New Haven and London: Yale University Press, 1977), 90–92.

    2. Arthur Hallam, "On Some of the Characteristics of Modern Poetry and on the *Lyrical Poems* of Alfred Tennyson," *The Englishman's Magazine* (1831), reprinted in *Victorian Poetry and Poetics,* ed. Walter E. Houghton and G. Robert Stange (Boston: Houghton Mifflin, 1968), 850, 856.

    3. W. J. Fox, review of Tennyson's *Poems, Chiefly Lyrical, Westminster Review* 14 (1831), reprinted in *Victorian Scrutinies,* ed. Isobel Armstrong (London: Athlone, 1972), 76.

    4. Ibid.

5. Ibid.

6. G. K. Chesteron, *Robert Browning* (London: Macmillan, 1903), 43.

7. Ibid, 202.

Part Three: Words of Power

1. Christopher Ricks, *Tennyson* (New York: Macmillan, 1972), 311.

Chapter Eleven

1. Walter Bagehot, "Wordsworth, Tennyson, and Browning; Or, Pure, Ornate, and Grotesque Art in English Poetry," in *Literary Studies,* ed. R. H. Hutton, vol. 2 (London; Longmans, 1898), 326–81. The essay was first published in 1864.

2. W. H. Auden, in *A Selection from the Poems of Alfred, Lord Tennyson* (Garden City, N.Y.: Doubleday, 1944), x.

3. G. K. Chesterton, *Robert Browning* (London: Macmillan, 1903), 115.

4. For a detailed analysis of Hegel's influence on E. S. Dallas and other Victorians see my discussion in "Hegel among the Poets: The Victorian Legacy," *The Lucid Veil* (London: Athlone, 1987), 234–40; also 232 and 253. The first Victorian review of Hegel's *Lectures on Aesthetics* comes as early as 1842 from G. H. Lewes. "Four years' constant study" of the master's *Lectures,* writes Hegel's ardent disciple, "has only served the more to impress me with its depth and usefulness." Lewes, "Hegel's Aesthetics; Philosophy of Art," *British and Foreign Review* 13 (1842), 42.

5. Alan Sinfield, *The Language of Tennyson's "In Memoriam"* (New York: Barnes and Noble, 1971), 105.

6. T. S. Eliot, *"In Memoriam,"* in *Selected Essays* (London: Faber and Faber, 1932), 333.

7. Herbert F. Tucker, Jr., *Tennyson and the Doom of Romanticism* (Cambridge, Mass.: Harvard University Press, 1988), 23.

Chapter Twelve

1. Helen Vendler, "Alternatives: The Reinvented Poem," *The Poetry of George Herbert* (Cambridge, Mass.: Harvard University Press, 1975), 25–56.

2. F. H. Bradley, *Aphorisms* (Oxford: Clarendon Press, 1930), aphorism 30.

3. James Richardson, *Vanishing Lives: Style and Self in Tennyson, D. G. Rossetti, Swinburne, and Yeats* (Charlottesville: University Press of Virginia, 1988), 90.

4. George Eliot, *Adam Bede,* ed. John Paterson (Boston: Houghton Mifflin, 1968), chap. 17, 151–52.

5. Richardson, 90.

6. Ibid., 32.

7. Ibid.

8.   A. S. Byatt, "The Conjugial Angel," *Angels and Insects: Two Novellas* (New York: Random House, 1992), 235.

Chapter Thirteen

1.   J. Hillis Miller, *Versions of Pygmalion* (Cambridge, Mass.: Harvard University Press, 1990), 101.

Chapter Fourteen

1.   Eric Griffiths, *The Printed Voice of Victorian Poetry* (Oxford: Clarendon Press, 1989), 132.
2.   Letter of Feb. 3, 1845, *The Letters of Robert Browning and Elizabeth Barrett 1845–1846,* ed. Elvan Kintner, vol. 1 (Cambridge, Mass.: Harvard University Press, 1969), 12–13. "This talking upon paper [is] as good a social pleasure as another, when our means are somewhat straightened."
3.   A. Dwight Culler, *The Poetry of Tennyson* (New Haven and London: Yale University Press, 1977), 96.
4.   Matthew Arnold, "On Translating Homer: Last Words," *The Complete Prose Works of Matthew Arnold,* ed. R. H. Super, vol. 1 (Ann Arbor, University of Michigan, 1960), 147.
5.   Griffiths, 209.
6.   Ralph Rader, "The Dramatic Monologue and Related Lyric Forms," *Critical Inquiry* 3 (1976), 136.
7.   G. S. Morson, "Dialogue, Monologue, and the Social," *Bakhtin: Essays and Dialogues on His Work* (Chicago and London: University of Chicago Press, 1986), 84.

Chapter Fifteen

1.   Stephen Booth, *King Lear, Macbeth, Indefinition, and Tragedy* (New Haven and London: Yale University Press, 1983), 15.
2.   Northrop Frye, *Anatomy of Criticism* (Princeton: Princeton University Press, 1957), 259.

Epilogue

1.   Douglas Bush, *Mythology and the Romantic Tradition in English Poetry* (Cambridge, Mass.: Harvard University Press, 1937), 226.

Bibliographical Essay

The definitive scholarly edition of Tennyson's work is the three-volume Longmans edition by Christopher Ricks, *The Poems of Tennyson* (London and Harlow: Longmans, Green, 1987), which collates the Eversely edition of Tennyson's *Works* (9 vols., Macmillan, 1907–1908) with the one-volume Macmillan edition of 1894. Ricks's three-volume edition of 1987 supersedes his earlier one-volume edition of 1969, which excludes quotations from the Trinity College MSS.

Supplementing Ricks's superbly executed contribution to Tennyson studies, which makes available a wealth of allusions and textual variants in its notes, is the three-volume edition of *The Letters of Alfred Lord Tennyson,* ed. Cecil Lang and Edgar F. Shannon, Jr. (Cambridge, Mass.: Harvard University Press, 1981, 1987, 1990). "An indifferent letter writer in prose," as one critic observes, "it is a miracle that [Tennyson] can perform the task so perfectly in verse" (Culler, 1977, 250). Unfortunately, of the few deeply felt letters in prose that he did write, including the ones to his fiancée Emily Sellwood, only a few fragments survive. And not a single letter remains of his correspondence with Arthur Hallam. Destroyed by Hallam's father, the letters to Arthur were most likely to have discussed poetry and ideas and to have been charged with the spontaneous enthusiasms and shared ambitions of a deep early friendship. Though less rewarding to read than the collected letters of Arnold, Clough, or Keats, the completed edition of Tennyson's letters remains an indispensable reference source.

The most balanced biography, *Alfred Tennyson* (New York: Macmillan, 1949), written by the poet's grandson Sir Charles Tennyson, makes excellent use of the Tennyson d'Eyncourt papers and reveals for the first time information about the drunkenness and violence of the poet's father. Such information had been withheld by Hallam Lord Tennyson in his earlier two-volume study, *Alfred Lord Tennyson: A Memoir* (London: Macmillan, 1897). On the control Tennyson exercises over his personal and literary reputation and over the materials he makes available to future biographers, readers should consult Michael Millgate's important study, *Testamentary Acts* (Oxford: Clarendon Press, 1992). The most recent and comprehensive biography of Tennyson, Robert Bernard Martin's *Tennyson: The Unquiet Heart* (New York: Oxford University

Press, 1980), errs, in my judgment, in the opposite direction from Hallam. If Tennyson's son verges on hagiography, turning "Alfred the Great (as he was known to his friends) into Alfred the king" (Lang and Shannon, p. xix), Martin diminishes Tennyson. He reduces Tennyson's fascination with dream states and trances to attacks of epilepsy and often sounds exasperated by religious beliefs he seems to think abnormal. Whereas Martin suffers from the limits of an imperfect sympathy and Hallam Tennyson is the adoring hagiographer, Charles Tennyson remains the more judicious biographer, a practioner of what one commentary calls "grandfilial candour and honesty" (Lang and Shannon, p. xxi).

Readers with an interest in feminist criticism should consult Marion Shaw's biographical-critical study, *Alfred Lord Tennyson: Feminist Readings* (Atlantic Highlands, N.J.: Humanities Press International, 1988). In his double view of female sexuality, which both attracts and repels him, Tennyson is revealed as a misogynist poet, even in *In Memoriam,* where we are shown why Sorrow and Nature are both female figures. Though the Tennyson who emerges from Shaw's study is no more admirable than Martin's Tennyson, the portrait she draws is more disturbing and original: its deft use of the psychological theories of Melanie Klein and Jacques Lacan also offers a greater challenge to future biographers.

In some quarters traditional literary criticism of Tennyson has been supplanted by theoretical studies that, in celebrating theory as its own reward, are critical but not literary; and by literary biographies or works of scholarship written under the banner of cultural studies that are literary but not critical. Notwithstanding, the number of Tennyson studies that continue to offer both literary and critical satisfaction would fill a bibliography many times longer than the present essay. In the following discussion of such studies I have selected only those books that have opened new depths of excitement for *me*. To trace recent changes in scholarship and criticism, I have also concentrated on books that represent both the old and new historicism and that include New Critical as well as more recent ideological studies of Tennyson's prodigious powers of language, where his claim to greatness surely lies.

For its depth of critical insight and breadth of learning few studies of Tennyson are likely to surpass A. Dwight Culler's *The Poetry of Tennyson* (New Haven and London: Yale University Press, 1977). Accessible to beginners, it is also a book to which the most learned Tennyson scholar can always return with profit and enjoyment.

Of traditional historical studies of Tennyson, the best accounts of the influence of classical authors are the brief but eloquent comments made by Douglas Bush in *Mythology and the Romantic Tradition in English Poetry* (Cambridge, Mass.: Harvard University Press, 1937), 202–24, and the authoritative monograph by Robert Pattison, *Tennyson and Tradition* (Cambridge, Mass.: Harvard University Press, 1979). George Ford's treatment of Tennyson's Romantic inheritance in his solid but modest monograph *Keats and the Victorians* (Hamden, Conn.: Yale University Press, 1962) has been superseded by Herbert F. Tucker's more ambitious and critically innovative study *Tennyson and the Doom of Romanticism* (Cambridge, Mass.: Harvard University Press, 1988).

Typical of the scholarship of the old historicism is Henry Kozicki's informed monograph *Tennyson and Clio: History in the Major Poems* (Baltimore: Johns Hopkins University Press, 1979), which traces the influence of Viconian and Hegelian philosophies of history on Tennyson. Kozicki is especially good on the "Liberal Anglican" historians who translated and diffused the thought of Barthold Niebuhr's *The History of Rome*.

A new historicist critic like Antony H. Harrison is more ambivalent about the influence of politics and literary history on Tennyson. In his chapter on *Maud* in *Victorian Poets and Romantic Poems: Intertextuality and Ideology* (Charlottesville: University Press of Virginia, 1990), Harrison argues that, depending on the biases of an 1855 reader, the poem could be viewed as advocating "either conservative or radical, or radically conservative, political values; a poem that presents a critique of the popular literary taste for Spasmodic poems, or one that embraces Spasmodic modes heartily" (89).

Two chapters of Gerhard Joseph's critically sophisticated book *Tennyson and the Text* (Cambridge: Cambridge University Press, 1992) bear the imprint of the new historicism. As in much of Stephen Greenblatt's writing, historical excursions that seem at first digressive prove to be points of entry into central topics. Professor Joseph's chapter on Julia Margaret Cameron's photography is not the anecdotal digression it first appears but a means of analyzing blurred effects in both Cameron's photography and Tennyson's verse. Nor is the chapter on Gladstone's and Tennyson's competition for Hallam's esteem a mere biographical trough between two high crests of theory. As Joseph shows, Gladstone's eccentric insistence on an intimate connection between biblical and Olympian revelations illuminates in a fresh and unexpected way the typology of Homeric type and Christian antitype in Tennyson's masterpiece, "Demeter and Persephone."

One of the few books on Tennyson to create and sustain a consistent thesis about the poet's anxieties is David Goslee's *Tennyson's Characters "Strange Faces, Other Minds"* (Iowa City: University of Iowa Press, 1989), which deserves to be better known. Goslee's demonstration of the skill with which Tennyson creates "a rich and varied fictional life outside the authorial self" (xv) is especially useful in accounting for the achievement of the poet's great monologues, his dramatic verse narratives, and his monodrama *Maud*. Just as versed in formalist analysis and deconstruction as in literary history and recent psychoanalytic theory, Goslee offers a sum of illuminating satifaction for which readers will be grateful.

Nina Auerbach's monograph, *Private Theatricals: The Lives of the Victorians* (Cambridge, Mass.: Harvard University Press, 1990) is only indirectly concerned with poetry. But its study of the impact of Victorian theatre and theatricality on such genres as the stage play, the dramatic monologue, and the elegy is subtle and steadily luminous and has important implications for Tennyson.

Since Tennyson is justly celebrated as a "lord of language," something should be said about the many books that study his poetic grammar, syntax, and ability to fine-tune the sounds and rhythms of words. For a sympathetic treatment of Tennyson's oblique use of words and his attempt to express, not merely the inexpressible, but also the inconceivable, readers should consult the last two chapters of F. E. L. Priestley's monograph, *Language and Structure in Tennyson's Poetry* (London: André Deutsch Ltd., 1973). Equally commendable for its imaginative study of Tennyson's poetic practice and knowledge of language theory is Donald S. Hair's wide-ranging book, *Tennyson's Language* (Toronto: University of Toronto Press, 1991). Arguing that "the fragment" is "the essential form" of *In Memoriam*, Hair shows how "this form is bound up with the language theories that lie behind the poem" (89). Addressing problems of structure and belief and "the deep mystery of [Tennyson's] spiritual regeneration" (7) in his monograph *Reading "In Memoriam"* (Princeton: Princeton University Press, 1985), Timothy Peltason offers a subtle and conceptually powerful reading of Tennyson's elegy. More circumscribed, though just as rewarding to read, are the first five chapters of James Richardson's book, *Vanishing Lives: Style and Self in Tennyson, D. G. Rossetti, Swinburne, and Yeats* (Charlottesville: University Press of Virginia, 1988). Richardson argues convincingly that Tennyson "is primarily an elegist of the *self*, and what he renders more fully than any other poet is the sense of life as transparent, ghostlike, dissolving, ungraspable, nearly unrememberable" (4). Using close stylistic and metrical analysis, Richardson gracefully discharges his self-set task of "explaining how poetry works and why it matters" (x).

Two exacting critical studies of Tennyson's language, which can find poetry in the most minimal elements of prosody and grammar, are Christopher Ricks's *Tennyson* (New York: Macmillan, 1972) [second edition published by University of California Press, Berkeley, in 1989], and Eric Griffith's chapter on Tennyson's breathing in *The Printed Voice of Victorian Poetry* (Oxford: Clarendon Press, 1989). No critic of Tennyson is more illuminating in his learned intuitions about off-rhymes, self-borrowings, and the poetic evocation of absence or silence, than Ricks. And Griffiths is unusually alert to the way reticences of the written word permit a reader to be nonpartisan by contemplating multiple meanings: breathing spaces on the printed page allow fractional truths to be declared and ampler sympathies to be felt.

The most comprehensive and convincing treatment of Tennyson and politics appears in Isobel Armstrong's large and luminous book, *Victorian Poetry: Poetry, Poetics, and Politics* (London: Routledge, 1994). Arguing that most Victorian poems are "double poems," which can be read in secretly politicized ways, she offers a brilliant analysis of Tennyson's conservative poetics of sensation, a category suggested by Arthur Hallam in his early review of his friend's volume, *Poems, Chiefly Lyrical*. Of equal grace and distinction are the analyses of Tennyson's language in Isobel Armstrong's *Language as Living Form in Nineteenth-Century Poetry* (Sussex: The Harvester Press, 1982). In studying *In Memoriam*'s habit of "sporting with words, its attempt to set the possibilities of metaphor in play" (204), her sixth chapter shows how Tennyson manages to erode idealist distinctions between subject and object by using ambiguous syntax and two-way meanings to fluctuate between mind-moulded and "matter-moulded" forms of speech.

Also exemplary in their demanding freshness of personal encounter is Alan Sinfield's monograph, *The Language of Tennyson's "In Memoriam"* (New York: Barnes and Noble, 1971), and his later Marxist study, *Alfred Tennyson* (Oxford: Blackwell, 1986). In his second book on Tennyson, Sinfield attempts a "materialist deconstruction" of the major poems in order to demonstrate the importance of what Fredric Jameson calls the "political unconscious." Whatever one may think of Sinfield's claim that the conflict between science and religion is no longer an issue for most educated people and his denial that *In Memoriam* represents a "unified self" (124), one can learn more from Sinfield when he seems wrong than from most critics when they are right. Readers will welcome Sinfield's lucid prose, his honest treatment of sexuality in Tennyson, and his responsiveness to what no amount of theorizing can disguise: the extraordinary subtlety and power of Tennyson's language, which explain why generations of readers keep returning to his poems with enduring satisfaction.

Bibliography

A list of all works cited in the text and bibliographical essay.

Ariès, Phillipe. *The Hour of Our Death*, trans. by Helen Weaver. New York: Knopf, 1981.

Armstrong, Isobel. *Victorian Poetry: Poetry, Poetics, and Politics*. London: Routledge, 1994.

————. *Language as Living Form in Nineteenth-Century Poetry*. Sussex: The Harvester Press, 1982.

Arnold, Matthew. "On Translating Homer: Last Words." *The Complete Prose Works of Matthew Arnold*, ed. R. H. Super, vol. 1. Ann Arbor: University of Michigan, 1960.

Auden, W. H. Introductory essay on Tennyson. In *A Selection from the Poems of Alfred, Lord Tennyson*. Garden City, N.Y.: Doubleday, 1944.

Auerbach, Nina. *Private Theatricals: The Lives of the Victorians*. Cambridge, Mass.: Harvard University Press, 1990.

Austin, J. L. *How to Do Things with Words*. Cambridge, Mass.: Harvard University Press, 1975.

Bagehot, Walter. "Wordsworth, Tennyson, and Browning; Or, Pure, Orante, and Grotesque Art in English Poetry." In *Literary Studies,* ed. R. H. Hutton, vol. 2. London; Longmans, 1898, 326–81.

Bal, Mieke. *Narratology: Introduction to the Theory of Narrative*. Toronto: University of Toronto Press, 1985.

Boone, Joseph Allen. *Tradition counter Tradition: Love and the Form of Fiction*. Chicago and London: University of Chicago Press, 1987.

Booth, Stephen *King Lear, Macbeth, Indefinition, and Tragedy*. New Haven and London: Yale University Press, 1983.

Bradley, F. H. *Aphorisms*. Oxford: Clarendon Press, 1930.

Browning, Robert. *The Letters of Robert Browning and Elizabeth Barrett Barrett 1845–1846,* ed. Elvan Kintner, vol. 1. Cambridge, Mass.: Harvard University Press, 1969.

Bush, Douglas. *Mythology and the Romantic Tradition in English Poetry*. Cambridge, Mass.: Harvard University Press, 1937.

————. "Alfred, Lord Tennyson." In *Major British Writers,* ed. G. B. Harrison. New York: Harcourt, Brace, 1954.

Byatt, A. S. "The Conjugial Angel." *Angels and Insects: Two Novellas*. New York: Random House, 1992.

Carlyle, Thomas. *The Works of Thomas Carlyle,* vol. 1. London: Chapman and Hall, 1898–1901.

Chesteron, G. K. *Robert Browning*. London: Macmillan, 1903.

Cixous, Hélène. *"Coming to Writing" and Other Essays,* ed. Deborah Jenson. Cambridge, Mass.: Harvard University Press, 1991.

Coveney, Peter, and Richard Highfield. *The Arrow of Time: A Voyage Through Science to Solve Time's Mystery*. New York: Fawcett Columbine, 1990.

Culler, A. Dwight. *The Poetry of Tennyson*. New Haven and London: Yale University Press, 1977.

Eliot, George. *Adam Bede*, ed. John Paterson. Boston: Houghton Mifflin, 1968.

Eliot, T. S. *"In Memoriam." Selected Essays*. London: Faber and Faber, 1932.

Empson, William "Tom Jones." *Using Biography*. Cambridge, Mass.: Harvard University Press, 1984.

Ferrier, J. F. *The Institutes of Metaphysics: Theory of Knowing and Being*. Edinburgh and London: Blackwood, 1854.

Ford, George. *Keats and the Victorians*. Hamden, Conn.: Yale University Press, 1962.

Fox, W. J. Review of Tennyson's *Poems, Chiefly Lyrical*. *Westminster Review* 14 (1831). Reprinted in Isobel Armstrong, ed. *Victorian Scrutinies* (London: Athlone, 1972).

Frye, Northrop. *Anatomy of Criticism*. Princeton: Princeton University Press, 1957.

———. *Words with Power*. New York: Harcourt Brace, 1990.

Goslee, David. *Tennyson's Characters "Strange Faces, Other Minds"*. Iowa City: University of Iowa Press, 1989.

Gray, J. M. *Thro' the Vision of the Night*. Montreal: McGill-Queen's Press, 1980.

Griffiths, Eric. *The Printed Voice of Victorian Poetry*. Oxford: Clarendon Press, 1989.

Hair, Donald S. *Tennyson's Language*. Toronto: University of Toronto Press, 1991.

Hallam, Arthur. "On Some of the Characteristics of Modern Poetry and on the *Lyrical Poems* of Alfred Tennyson." *The Englishman's Magazine* (1831). Reprinted in *Victorian Poetry and Poetics*, ed. Walter E. Houghton and G. Robert Stange. Boston: Houghton Mifflin, 1968.

Harrison, Antony H. *Victorian Poets and Romantic Poems: Intertextuality and Ideology*. Charlottesville: University Press of Virginia, 1990.

Jarrell, Randall. *Poetry and the Age*. New York: Knopf, 1953.

Joseph, Gerhard. *Tennysonian Love: The Strange Diagonal*. Minneapolis: University of Minnesota Press, 1969.

———. *Tennyson and the Text*. Cambridge: Cambridge University Press, 1992.

Keble, John. *Lectures on Poetry, 1832–1841,* trans. E. K. Francis, vol. 2. Oxford: Clarendon Press, 1912.

Kierkegaard, Søren. *Stages on Life's Way*, trans. David F. Svenson and Walter Lowrie. Princeton: Princeton University Press, 1940.

Kozicki, Henry. *Tennyson and Clio: History in the Major Poems*. Baltimore: Johns Hopkins University Press, 1979.

Lewes, G. H. "Hegel's Aesthetics; Philosophy of Art." *British and Foreign Review* 13 (1842).

Mansel, H. L. *The Limits of Religious Thought Examined in Eight Lectures*. Bampton Lectures for 1858. London: J. Murray, 1867.

Martin, Robert. *Tennyson: The Unquiet Heart*. New York: Oxford University Press, 1980.

Miller, J. Hillis. *Versions of Pygmalion*. Cambridge, Mass.: Harvard University Press, 1990.

Millgate, Michael. *Testamentary Acts: Browning, Tennyson, James, Hardy*. Oxford: Clarendon Press, 1992.

Morson, G. S. "Dialogue, Monologue, and the Social." *Bakhtin: Essays and Dialogues on His Work*. Chicago and London: University of Chicago Press, 1986.

Pattison, Robert. *Tennyson and Tradition*. Cambridge, Mass.: Harvard University Press, 1979.

Peltason, Timothy. *Reading "In Memoriam"*. Princeton: Princeton University Press, 1985.

Potok, Chaim. *The Chosen*. New York: Fawcett Crest, 1967.

Priestley, F. E. L. *Language and Structure in Tennyson's Poetry*. London: André Deutsch Ltd., 1973.

Rader, Ralph. "The Dramatic Monologue and Related Lyric Forms." *Critical Inquiry* 3 (1976).

Reed, John R. *Perception and Design in Tennyson's 'Idylls of the King'*. Athens: Ohio University Press, 1969.

Richardson, James. *Vanishing Lives: Style and Self in Tennyson, D. G. Rossetti, Swinburne, and Yeats*. Charlottesville: University Press of Virginia, 1988.

Ricks, Christopher. *Tennyson*. New York: Macmillan, 1972, 2d ed. Berkeley: University of California Press, 1989.

———. "The Antithetical Sense." *Beckett's Dying Words*. Oxford: Oxford University Press, 1993, 128–45.

Rosenberg, John D. *The Fall of Camelot: A Study of Tennyson's 'Idylls of the King'*. Cambridge, Mass.: Harvard University Press, 1973.

Ryals, Clyde de L. *From the Great Deep: Essays on 'Idylls of the King'*. Athens, Ohio: Ohio University Press, 1973.

Sartre, Jean-Paul. "Bad Faith." In *Being and Nothingness*, trans. Hazel E. Barnes. New York: Washington Square Press, 1966.

Shaw, Marion. *Alfred Lord Tennyson: Feminist Readings*. Atlantic Highlands, N.J.: Humanities Press International, 1988.

Shaw, W. David. "Hegel among the Poets: The Victorian Legacy." *The Lucid Veil*. London: Athlone, 1987.

Sidney, Philip. *An Apologie for Poetrie*, ed. J. Churton Collins. Oxford: Clarendon Press, 1950.

Sinfield, Alan. *The Language of Tennyson's "In Memoriam"*. New York: Barnes and Noble, 1971.

————. *Alfred Tennyson*. Oxford: Blackwell, 1986.

Stoppard, Tom. *Rosencrantz and Guildenstern are Dead*. London: Faber and Faber, 1967.

Tennyson, Lord Alfred. *The Works of Tennyson,* ed. Hallam Lord Tennyson, vols. 8 and 9. London: Macmillan, 1908.

————. *The Poems of Tennyson,* ed. Christopher Ricks, 3 vols. London and Harlow: Longmans, Green, 1987.

————. *The Letters of Alfred Lord Tennyson,* ed. Cecil Lang and Edgar F. Shannon Jr., 3 vols. Cambridge, Mass.: Harvard University Press, 1981, 1987, 1990.

Tennyson, Sir Charles. *Alfred Tennyson*. New York: Macmillan, 1949.

Tennyson, Hallam. *Alfred Lord Tennyson: A Memoir,* 2 vols. London: Macmillan, 1897.

Tucker, Herbert F., Jr. *Tennyson and the Doom of Romanticism*. Cambridge, Mass.: Harvard University Press, 1988.

Vendler, Helen. "Alternatives: The Reinvented Poem." *The Poetry of George Herbert*. Cambridge, Mass.: Harvard University Press, 1975, 25–56.

Wilde, Oscar. *De Profundis*. New York, Vintage, 1964.

Wollheim, Richard. *The Thread of Life*. Cambridge, Mass.: Harvard University Press, 1984.

Yeats, W. B. "Edmund Spenser." In *Essays and Introductions*. New York: Collier, 1961.

Index

Italics indicate a main discussion.

Frye, Northrop, 54, 153–54

"Gardener's Daughter, The," (Tennyson), 8–9
genre: allegory, 46, 59, 155; beast fable, 20; burlesque, 21; closet drama, 146; confessional elegy, 32; disturbing or transforming genres, 25–35, 46–59, 157; dramatic lyric, 101; dramatic monologue, 61–75, 82, 89–99, 156, 158, 170; dramatic monologue, theory of, 100–104, 136, 137–47; dramatic monologue versus stage play, 66–69, 76–81, 100–101, 137, 146–47; elegy, 1, 25, 31–45, 70, 170; epic, 1, 28–30, 46–59; experiments with genre, 1; fairy tale, 11; "gallery poem," 19; idyll, 8–9; interior monologue, 79; lyrical monologue, 67; masked love poem, 11; melodrama, 87, 95; monodrama, 15, 61, 82; narrative displacements of a lyric impulse, 4; narrative poetry, 1, 3; ode, 25–26, 110, 135–36, 148–49; poetry of state, 25–28, 158; psalm, 110; romance, 47; satire, 1, 22; soliloquy, 66, 137, 140; verse epistle, 1
Gladstone, William Ewart, 28, 169
Godwin, William, 27
Goslee, David, 170
grammar: appositional, 40, 133, 137–38, 154; auxiliary verbs of volition, 91; dissolution of grammar, 113; double meanings, 105, 134–36, 138–39, 140, 171; double negative, 74; ellipsis, 44, 93, 116, 124, 135, 137; parallel syntax, 54; paratactic syntax, 144, 157; parities of syntax, 66; self-embedding syntax, 108; solecism, 3; subjective and objective genitives, 16, 120; tenseless infinitives, 134; two-way syntax, 16, 122
Gray, Thomas, 40
Greenblatt, Stephen, 169
Griffiths, Eric, 137, 146, 171

Hair, Donald S., 170

Hallam, Arthur, 4, 35–36, 70, 100–4, 124, 151, 157, 167, 169, 171
Hamilton, Sir William, 121
Hardy, Thomas, 28, 139
Harrison, Antony H., 169
Hegel, Georg Wilhelm Friedrich, 109
Herbert, George, 119
"Hesperides, The," (Tennyson), 73, 89–90, 93–94
"Higher Pantheism, The," (Tennyson), 120
Homer, 89, 142, 144
Hooker, Richard, 27
Hopkins, Gerard Manley, 116
Horace, 25, 158

Idylls of the King, 11–13, 25, 29–30, 36, 46–59, 71, 155, 158; "Balin and Balan," 49, 52; "Coming of Arthur, The," 11–13, 46–47; "Gareth and Lynette," 47–48; "Geraint and Enid," 48–49; "Guinevere," 50–51, 54, 58–59; "Holy Grail, The," 30, 54, 103; "Lancelot and Elaine," 52, 68–69; "Last Tournament, The," 29, 55–58; "Marriage of Geraint, The," 48; "Passing of Arthur, The," 12, 29, 40, 43, 72, 149–51; "Pelleas and Ettarre," 49, 53; "To the Queen," 58, 155
"In the Garden at Swainston," 123–25
In Memoriam, 1, 4, 28, 31–35, 36, 70, 101, 171–72; section 7, 112–13, 122; section 9, 33; section 10, 128–29; section 12, 33–34, 151; section 47, 157; section 54, 95; sections 54–56, 114–15; section 86, 107–9, 122; section 95, 44, 116–18; section 101, 15–16, 127–28; section 121, 134–35; section 123, 113–14, 123; section 124, 120–21; section 130, 156–57
irony, 17, 67, 86, 88–89, 103, 132, 136, 141–42, 144–45; single and double irony, 63; double irony, 71

James, Henry, 18
Jameson, Fredric, 171
Jarrell, Randall, 42

About the Author

A graduate of Harvard University and a Fellow of the Royal Society of Canada, W. David Shaw is professor of English at Victoria College, University of Toronto. A skeptical questioner (rather than an uncritical apologist) of recent literary theories, he has written an earlier monograph, *Tennyson's Style* (Cornell University Press, 1976), and numerous articles on the poet. His other books include *Elegy and Paradox: Testing the Conventions* (Johns Hopkins University Press, 1994), *Victorians and Mystery: Crises of Representation* (Cornell University Press, 1990), *The Lucid Veil: Poetic Truth in the Victorian Age* (Athlone and Wisconsin, 1987), and *The Dialectical Temper: The Rhetorical Art of Robert Browning* (Cornell University Press, 1968).